The Big Book of Paper Crafting

Great Uses For Your Scrapbooking Tools

The Designers

We are grateful to the following people for creating the projects which appear in this book, and we're proud to spotlight their work. In alphabetical order, they are:

- Sandy Bunka
- Helen Deinema
- Bonnie Dunkel
- LeNae Gerig
- Marilyn Gossett
- Becky Goughnour
- Katie Hacker

- Linda Ippel
- Caryl McHarney
- Tammi Schroeder
- Eunice Sherwood
- Anne-Marie Spencer
- Deborah Spofford
- Stephanie Taylor

The publisher and designers would like to thank the following companies for providing materials used in this publication:

- **Accent Design** for wood buttons
- **Accu/Cut® Systems** for die cuts
- **Adhesive Technologies, Inc.** for Craft & Floral Pro low temperature glue gun & sticks
- **American Oak Preserving Co., Inc.** for raffia and dried floral materials
- **Artifacts, Inc.** for paper doilies
- **The Beadery®** for beads
- **C.M. Offray & Son, Inc.** for ribbons
- **Creative Beginnings** for brass charms
- **DC&C** for corrugated journals, papier-mâché and jute twine
- **DMD Industries, Inc.** for cardstock and Paper Reflections spiral-bound books
- **DecoArt** for acrylic paints
- **Delta Technical Coatings, Inc.** for acrylic paints, sealers and decoupage glue
- **Duncan Enterprises** for Aleene's® tacky craft glue and reverse decoupage glue
- **EK Success Ltd.** for Zig® pens and glues
- **Elmer's®** for adhesives and decoupage glue
- **Family Treasures** for scissors and punches
- **Fiskars®, Inc.** for straight and decorative scissors, corner edgers and circle cutter
- **Forster, Inc.®** for Woodsies™ wood shapes and craft sticks
- **Frances Meyer®, Inc.** for stickers
- **The Gifted Line®** for stickers
- **Hiller** for spiral-bound books
- **Hot Off The Press, Inc.** for Paper Pizazz™ papers, Punch-Outs™ and Cards with Pizazz

- **Hunt** for photo mats
- **Hygloss Products, Inc.** for gold metallic and velour papers, foil board and paper doilies
- **KITI** for Cool Shades lampshade kits
- **Lara's Crafts** for wood knobs
- **Lion Ribbon Co.** for ribbons and trims
- **Loose Ends** for handmade papers
- **MPR Associates, Inc.** for Paperbilities™ papers, velour posterboard, tissue paper and paper ribbon
- **Marvy® Uchida** for punches and pens
- **McGill, Inc.** for scissors and punches
- **Mrs. Grossman's Paper Co.** for stickers
- **One & Only Creations®** for doll hair
- **Paper Patch®** for papers
- **Provo Craft®** for stickers
- **RubberStampede®** for rubber stamps
- **Stampendous!** for rubber stamps
- **StenSource Int'l., Inc.** for stencils
- **Vaban Gille, Inc.** for gold angel hair
- **Walnut Hollow** for wood products
- **Wrights** for ribbons, self-adhesive ribbons and ribbon roses

Hot Off The Press Production Credits:

Project editors:	Mary Margaret Hite, Tara Choate
Technical editor:	LeNae Gerig
Photographer:	Reed Anderson
Graphic designers:	Jacie Pete, Susan Shea
Digital imagers:	Victoria Gleason, Larry Seith
Editors:	Paulette Jarvey, Kris Andrews
	Lynda Hill, Tom Muir

published by **LEISURE ARTS® CRAFT LEAFLETS**

P.O. Box 55595
Little Rock, Arkansas 72215

produced by
HOT OFF THE PRESS INC.

Canby, Oregon USA

Library of Congress catalog number 98-94155
ISBN 1-57486-081-X

Styrofoam® is a registered trademark of the Dow Chemical Company

The Big Book of
Paper Crafting

Great Uses For Your Scrapbooking Tools

Tips & Tools

Paper 6
Cardstock 7
Specialized Papers 7
Scissors 8
Glue 8
Pens 8
Craft Knife 9
Corrugator 9
Stylus 9
Glue Gun 9
Shoestring Bow 9
Wrappings 10
Embellishments 10
Stickers, Die Cuts & Punch-Outs™..11
Punches 11

Cheerful, Clever, Charming Cards

Making & Covering Cards 14
Making Envelopes 15
Pocket Cards 16–17
  Balloon Card in Gift Pocket 16
  Bee Happy 16
  Congratulations! 16
  "Buttons" 17
  Hungry Frog 17
  Quilt Card 17
Shaker Box Cards 18–19
  Hydrangea Garden Card 18
  Christmas Plaid Card 19
  "It's a Boy" Card 19
Gold Crinkle Card 19
3-D Cards 20
  "Welcome Home" Card 20
  Trick-or-Treat Card & Envelope 20
Cutaway Card 21
Bi-Fold Ballerina Card 21

Invitations & Announcements

Cards with Die Cuts 24–26
  Balloon Birthday Invitation 24
  Super Bowl Party 24
  Open House 25

Ice Cream Party 25
Graduation Party 26
Baby Announcement 26
It's a Girl! 27
It's a Boy! 27
Lacy Formals 28
  Laser-printed Invitation 28
  Hand-lettered Invitation 28
Lacy Heart Engagement Card 28
Announcement with Lace Envelope..29
Pop-Up Party Card 29
Haunted House 30

It's in the Bag

Mini Gift Bags 34–36
  Burgundy Bag 34
  Floral Paper Bag 34
  Blue Corrugated Bag 34
  Ivory Sachet Bag 34
  Dogwood Bag..........................35
  Roses & Raffia Bag 35
  Ho Ho Ho Bag 36
  Plaid Bag with Lid 36
Pleated Gift Folders 36–39
  Pink Roses Folder 36
  Christmas Folders 37
  Snowflake Envelopes.................37
  Birthday Folder 38
  Hearts & Kisses 38
  Lacy Pleated Folder 38
  Floral Folder with "Lace" Trim ..39
Flat Folders............................39
Embellished Bags 40–41
  "Bronze" Star Bag 40
  Heart Friend Bag 40
  Tuxedo Bag 40
  Watermelon Bag 41
  Diagonal Dots Bag....................41
Animal Bags............................42–45
  Bunnies.................................42
  Dog......................................42
  Bear 43
  Panda 43
  Kitty 44
  Frog 44
Halloween Bags 46–48
  Ghost 46
  Jack-O-Lantern 46
  Monstro 47
  Black Cat 47
  Scarecrow 48

Haunted Graveyard 48
Christmas Bags 49–51
  Reindeer..............................49
  Penguin...............................49
  Snowman 50
  Santa 50
  Elf 51
Terrific Tags 52–53
  Triple-Fold Tags 52
  Layered Tags 53
  Folded Tags 53

Present-Perfect Boxes

Nesting Boxes 56–57
Boxes from Cards 58–59
  Ice Cream & Candles 58
  Tie Dye & Raffia 58
  "You're Great" 58
  Antique Lace Box 59
  Trims & Doilies 59
  Hydrangeas Box 59
  Green Marble Box 59
Shaker-Top Boxes....................60–61
  Rose Box & Variations 60
  Blue Corrugated Box.................61
  Christmas House Box 61
Gift Pockets............................62
Square Fold-Ups 63

Home Decor with Style & More

Decoupage Plates 66
  Heart Plate............................66
  Star Plate..............................66
  Polka Dot Plate.......................66
  Striped Plate..........................66
Decoupage Frames 67
Decoupage Candle Holder 67
Reverse Decoupage Rose Set........68
Dainty Doily Pot 68
Triangle Letter Box 69
Angel Saucer...........................69
Children's Easy
  Decoupage Dresser Set 70–71
Mosaic Terra Cotta Pot...............72
Mosaic Fish Tray........................72
Corrugated Wall Hanging..............73
Corrugated Box........................73

Quilted Welcome Wall Hanging 74
Pastel Wall Quilt 75
Fall Leaves Hanging 75
Seasonal Photo Mats..............76–77
    Spring 76
    Summer 76
    Autumn 76
    Winter 77
    Dogwood Mat 77
    Ladybugs Mat 77
Cream Velvet Box........................78
Velvet Lampshade 79
Pink Gingham Frame 79
Paper Rose Projects.....................80
Rose Frame 81
Green Wood Frame 82
Triptych Wall Hanging 82
Magnets......................................83

Journals & Books

Mini Gift Books 86–87
    Always & Forever 86
    Dear Friend 87
    Happy Birthday.........................87
Mini Photo Albums 88–89
    Amanda & Auntie Lynda...........88
    Generations 89
    Sunflowers 89
Accordion-Fold Books..............90–91
    Sticks & Bands 90
    Elk Lake 91
    Bubbles Thank You Book...........91
Books from Cards....................92–93
    Gran's Brag Book 92
    Just Wanted to Tell You 93
    You Remain an Original...........93
Square Books 94–95
    Pink Roses Book 92
    Baby Book 93
    Hydrangeas Book 93
    Bridal Book 93
To the Sea 96
Old Letters Scrapbook..................96
Victorian Scrapbook 97
Vintage Photo Journal 97
Baby Book 98
Hugs & Kisses 98
Holly Leaf Christmas Book 99
Fisherman's Brag Book 99
Americana Journal 100
Little Fern Book 100
Hydrangeas & Cherub 101
Sunny Reflections 101

Paper Treasures & Holiday Pleasures

Puffy Ornaments 104
Tree Box 105
Heart Ornament 105
Christmas Wall Cards.................106
Happy Holidays Hanging............106
Angel Topiaries.........................107
Angel Hanging..........................108
Angel Tree Topper 108
Heart Ornament 109
Fan Ornaments 109
Snowflake Ornament.................109

Gifts, Presents & Splendid Surprises

Seed Packet Sachets...................112
    Lavender Heart Sachet 112
    Love Heart Sachet 112
    Ballerina Sachet 112
    Vellum Fern Sachet 112
    Pink Rose Sachet 112
    Quilt Sachet 112
Flower Girl Hangers 113
Pockets Full of Love 114–115
    Quilting Grandma 114
    Heartstrings.............................114
    Window Cards with Sachets ...115
Stuffed Paper Ornaments 116–117
    "Quilted" Angel 116
    Apple for the Teacher..............116
    Plaid Teddy Bear 117
Stationery Packets 118
    Pink Roses Folder....................118
    Flowers & Lace 118
    Holly Folder 118
    Plaid & Gingerbread................118
    Pine & Lights 118
Bookmarks 119
Photo Pin & Card 119
Paper Brooches 120
    Heart Brooch 120
    Button Pin 120
    Seashell Brooch 120
    Corrugated Oval 120
Pin Gift Folders........................121
    Love Folder with Heart Pin......121
    Blue Folder with Rose Pin 121
    Black Folder with Beehive Pin ..121

Paper Bead Necklaces 122
    Suede Choker 122
    Green & Peach Necklace 122
    Blue and Brown Necklace.......122
    Purple & Gold Necklace 122
Mom's Box.................................123
Fern Box & Cards 123

Pretty Paper Party Favors

Triangle Boxes 126
Birdhouse Box 127
Christmas House Box..................127
Heart Basket & Box 128
Pink Round Box.........................128
Pink Lace Purse 129
Bridal Lace Sachet 129
Paper Ribbon Angel 130
Paper Ribbon Bath Sachet 130
Birthday Bunny 131

Rubber Stamping & Fun for Everyone

Stamping Basics 134
Cleaning Stamps 134
Sponging...................................134
Embossing.................................134
Masking....................................134
Cutting Windows 134
3-Dimensional Supports 134
Pop-Up Placecard 135
    3-D Birthday Card...................135
    Postcard Invitation 135
Christmas Cheer 136
A Tree in the Window 136
Garden Angel Card.....................137
    I Love You 137
    Thank You 137
Vellum-Lined Windows...............138
    Poppy Card 138
    Nasturtium Card 138
Apple Harvest 139
    Wheelbarrow Card 139
    Dried Flowers Card 139
Seashore Thanks........................140
Lighthouse Bag 140

Patterns 141–143
Index 144

In this book you'll find that paper doesn't have to simply lie flat! It can bend and twist and become a box, or a bag, or a terrific party favor!

Paper can be made into some really great gifts, as you'll see in the chapter *Gifts, Presents & Splendid Surprises*. It can also elegantly decorate or create books and journal covers as shown in *Journals & Books*. Paper crafts also can be featured throughout your home with the designs in *Home Decor with Style & More*. You'll see many types

of Christmas crafts made from paper in *Paper Treasures & Holiday Pleasures*. And you'll be amazed at the number of designs this book offers for making cards, invitations and announcements with just paper, a few punches and a pair of decorative scissors! Of course, the book just wouldn't be complete without some really fun ideas for crafting *Present-Perfect Boxes* or gift bags and tags. And if you have even one party to throw this year, the *Pretty Paper Party Favors* chapter will help turn your table into a celebration display!

As a nice surprise for readers who make memory albums, all your scrapbooking tools do double duty in papercrafting. As you page through this book you'll see paper punches, patterned scissors and die cuts, as well as solid and patterned papers. So get out your scrapbooking tools, but set aside your photos for now...these paper crafts give you a whole new use for your tools!

Paper From mat board to tissue, "paper" is the catch-all term used to refer to the many types that are used in this craft. Each kind provides a different look or feel to a design. Some designs call for a heavyweight paper, some call for lightweight paper. Here, you'll see different types of paper and read about specific uses for each one.

The paper used as the primary material in most of these projects is of medium weight—60# or 70# paper that is heavier than tracing paper, or the thickness of the average stationery or scrapbooking paper. Slightly thinner,

lightweight paper is about the thickness of notebook paper, and slightly thicker, or heavyweight, paper is the thickness of construction paper.

Patterned paper is a perfect way to provide color in your projects. It can provide patterns and theme to a project where before there was none. You will get quite a different project simply by altering the papers used. For instance, muted maroon, blue or plaid papers can lend a country look to a project, while bold colors, in solids or patterns, used for the same project offer more of a contemporary look.

Cardstock

Cardstock is thicker than construction paper but not as heavy as cardboard. Its thickness can vary from that of a manila folder to that of posterboard. It is sold in 8½"x11" sheets or as pre-folded blank cards.

Cardstock isn't just for making cards! It can make a brag book such as the one on page 92, or be crafted into the backing for a beautiful brooch (page 120). Cardstock is great for projects that call for heavy paper such as boxes, gift bags or cards. It can take the place of wood when making a plaque, or of cardboard when constructing a box.

You can draw on or color white cardstock, or use a solid-colored piece. You may want to cut a pattern for a project from white cardstock, then cover it with patterned paper. Or use a patterned piece of cardstock—new to the market. There are plenty of options available to create many wonderful projects, as you'll soon see.

Specialized Papers

There are projects in this book that use specific papers to create a unique design. For example, corrugated paper is used to craft a country wall hanging, page 73, and doily paper is used to make the tree topper design on page 108.

Handmade paper is often used as an embellishment in papercrafting. A torn edge reinforces the handmade feel of this paper. To tear handmade paper, fold the edge and lightly moisten it before tearing.

Tissue paper is used in the decoupage projects on pages 66–72. Also, it's a great "wrapping" paper for use inside gift bags, as you'll see in the chapter *It's in the Bag*. On page 80 you'll find instructions on how to make a tissue paper rose.

Glossy and metallic papers create a rich effect as shown in the projects on pages 40 and 41. The sparkling surface of metallic or glossy papers produces a gleaming look in these projects.

Tools Along with paper for paper crafts, you'll need scissors, glue and pens. You can make tons of projects with just these three tools.

Scissors Straight-edged scissors are the only kind you'll actually **need** to craft with paper, but it's nice to have at least two lengths—short, sharp-pointed scissors for details, and longer shears to make the work go faster when you have a lot of cutting to do. It's best to keep the scissors in one position and move the paper as you cut out a pattern or shape.

Decorative scissors have patterned edges, and are the first "extra" most papercrafters invest in. Many different looks can be achieved with the switch of a blade. By turning the scissors upside down, you can get a mirror-image effect.

The shaker cards on pages 20 and 21 use decorative cuts on the windows to add interest and enhance the different themes.

Glue Clear-drying glue will provide the clean look you'll want for each of these designs. It can be found in stick, pen, spray or liquid form. Pen or stick glues work well when you need only a small amount to secure the paper in place. When covering cardstock with patterned paper, use a thin layer of spray adhesive to get a smooth look, or paint on a thin layer of diluted tacky craft glue. A glue gun or tacky craft glue offer extra strength for projects using cardboard, wood or metal, or for attaching heavy embellishments such as charms.

The decoupage and reverse collage projects (see pages 66–72) require their own special glues. Follow the manufacturer's instructions to apply each. Also, a thin layer of decoupage glue works well when a project needs a sealer.

Double-stick tape is another way to attach paper. Double-sided foam mounting tape also provides depth to various parts of your projects. It's available in strips, squares or dots.

Pens Throughout the book you'll find projects that use a pen to write a message or draw a picture. Pens provide an easy way to add a simple border around a frame (page 77) or a message inside a book (page 93).

Different types of pens will produce different effects on different papers. For instance, metallic pens complement glossy papers, while opaque pens show up well on contrasting backgrounds. Pens also create different effects within a design. While ball-point pens come in many colors and can offer a casual feel, calligraphy pens have a wide squared tip that can give an elegant, shaded look to letters and lines. Be sure the ink is color-fast if a glue or sealer is to be used over it. You don't want the ink to smear your perfect paper craft!

Extras

Besides the basic materials, a few extras are nice to have. Below you'll find some tips on how to use them most effectively.

Craft Knife

A craft knife, or X-acto® knife, works well when cutting inside a window or along a straight edge or guide. It will allow you to cut those tiny details without making mistakes. Use a self-healing mat, a cutting board or a piece of cardboard underneath to protect your work surface.

Corrugator

Corrugated paper adds depth and texture to your paper crafts. If you can't find just the right color of corrugated paper, or want to corrugate a piece of patterned cardstock or paper, this tool can give you exactly what you want! Insert the paper into the rollers, turn the handle and let the paper come out the other side.

Stylus

A stylus is used to score paper or cardstock to make it easy to fold along a straight line. Simply lay a ruler on the paper along the line you want to fold and press the stylus into the paper, drawing the tool along the edge of the ruler. Be careful when scoring thin paper as it tears more easily.

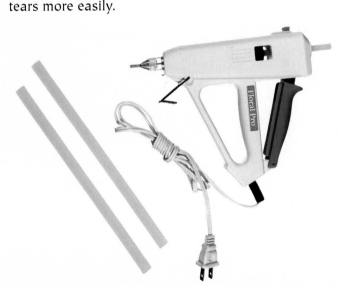

Glue Gun

Glue guns and sticks are a practical alternative to tacky craft glue. If you already have one, it'll work well for tacking heavier embellishments on your projects. Since the glue is bulky, avoid a glue gun when you need a thin, smooth application. Remember to use caution when using a glue gun if small children are present. Even a low-temperature glue gun can burn!

Shoestring Bow

Many closures and decorations throughout this book are shoestring bows. Tie the ribbons much like you tie your shoes. To adjust the size of the loops, pull on the tails, then pull the loops in opposite directions to tighten. Trim each tail diagonally; it's optional to knot each tail.

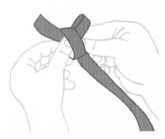

Additionals

Include some extra supplies in your paper-crafting to achieve very intriguing and elegant results. The list of "additionals" is quite extensive; here are some of them and how they can be used to make the most of your paper crafts!

Wrappings

Many projects have bows, are tied closed with ribbon, use raffia handles, or are hung with ribbon, cord, twine or wire.

The ribbons and cords used in this book vary from 1mm to 2" wide. The size of the project and the delicacy of the effect desired determine the correct width.

Twine also comes in different widths. It's used for its strength, but its natural look lends a country feel to a project.

Raffia gives a country, garden or natural feel to any project. It's sold curly or straight and comes natural or dyed in various colors. You can shred the strands with your fingernail to get a finer width or fluffier appearance.

Paper ribbon adds a natural feel while still offering an elegant decoration. It, too, comes in many widths and colors in a wide array of printed patterns. Some is sold twisted into a cord and can be used as is, or untwisted for an attractive crinkly flat ribbon.

Embellishments

Embellishing your project is perhaps the most fun of creating your paper craft! It's easy to add a personal touch to these projects when you use some of the enhancements shown here.

Beads strung on wire or twine lend a country or natural feel to the project. This effect is used in projects in the *Home Decor* section as well as elsewhere in the book.

Charms are used in many projects in the book. You'll see that, glued on or hung with ribbon, they create a sense of elegance in a design.

Wood pieces lend texture to your project. They can be painted with acrylic colors and sealed before using in the project.

Glitter or confetti adds fun and a gleaming sparkle to whatever it adorns! And using dried or silk flowers is a perfect way to include a bit of the garden in these crafts.

Stickers, Die Cuts and Punch-Outs™

Stickers are convenient to use because they're self-adhesive and come in so many styles. They're available in many shapes, sizes and themes so it's easy to find decorative elements to quickly complete your paper craft.

Die cuts are paper shapes cut with metal forms called "dies." They're handy because you can cut the shape you want from any paper you like. Most paper crafting stores have die-cutting machines and dies. They can cut the pattern you want with any paper you provide. The machines are able to cut multiple papers at the same time; this makes it easy when you need many of the same die patterns.

Punch-Outs™ are a super-simple way to embellish any project. They're sold in themed books found in most papercrafting stores. They're larger than stickers but aren't adhesive, so you can move them around till their placement is perfect without worrying about ruining your project.

Punches

Not only do punches make great embellishments, they make great paper crafts, too! Punches make it easy to add decorative and fun elements to any design.

Punches are used to create terrific frames in our *Home Decor with Style & More* chapter. They're used as embellishments to make *Cheerful, Clever, Charming Cards*, and you'll be amazed at the *Gifts, Presents & Splendid Surprises* that use punches for decorations! Throughout this book, you'll see punches used liberally as quick and easy enhancements for bags, boxes, journals, frames and more!

Besides squeeze punches such as hole punches, push punches are popular for papercrafting. They work better for larger or more detailed shapes and they're easy to use! Just set the punch on a hard surface, like a table, slip your paper into the slot and push down on the top with the heel of your hand.

To sharpen your punch, punch a piece of fine-grained sand paper. To lubricate a punch, punch a piece of waxed paper.

Cheerful, Clever, Charming Cards

Believe it or not, there are more than seven billion cards sent out to friends and family members each year! We send cards to say anything from "Cheer Up!" to "You mean so very much to me," to "Happy Birthday!" For these very special occasions, people or sentiments, we want a card that will convey what we want to express in just the way that we want to express it.

Handmade cards give us the ability to do just that. The thought and planning that goes into something we've made just for one special person is much better than anything a card company could write. The love, friendship and warm feelings that inspire us are what make handcrafted cards so appreciated.

This chapter will give you plenty of ideas on how to make such a card and tailor it for any occasion. Punches, patterned papers, cardstock, Punch-Outs™ or stickers can be used to craft your message of friendship.

Best of all, with the directions in this book, you can express your sense of caring to the people around you in a very personal way.

Making & Covering Cards

Pre-folded cards with matching envelopes are available in a variety of sizes, styles and finishes. However, if you can't find just what you're looking for, it's easy to make a card from a piece of cardstock. You'll need a ruler, a pencil and a stylus or embossing tool.

1. **Making your own card:** Cut the cardstock to the correct height and twice the width you want your finished card to be (for a top-folded card, the correct width and twice the height). On the back side, measure and lightly pencil the fold line down the card center.

2. Lay the ruler along the fold line and hold it firmly in place. Run the stylus along the ruler edge, pressing down firmly to score a groove in the cardstock.

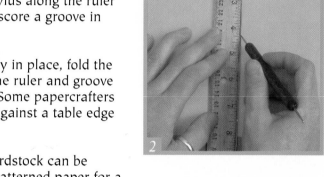

3. Still holding the ruler firmly in place, fold the card on the scored line. The ruler and groove help to create a smooth fold. (Some papercrafters prefer to hold the scored line against a table edge for folding.)

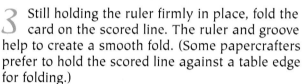

4. **Covering a card:** Plain cardstock can be covered with textured or patterned paper for a different look (or recycle old cards with new coverings). Spray adhesive produces the smoothest results; you can also apply diluted tacky craft glue with a paintbrush. Spread newspapers to protect your work surface. Open the card and lay it front side up on the newspaper; lay the patterned paper wrong side up in another area. Spray the card with an even coat of adhesive.

5. Pick the card up by the center, allowing it to fold halfway closed, and move it onto the patterned paper. Press the back of the card firmly in place, then fold the paper to the front, smoothing it in place. (*Note:* Many spray adhesives can be used to produce either a temporary or a permanent bond. Be sure to read the label instructions for the brand you are using.)

6. **Lining a card:** To line the entire inside of a card with paper, cut the paper slightly smaller (at least 1/16") than the card inside and fold it before spraying it. Insert it carefully into the half-open card and smooth it in place from the fold to the edges. Sometimes only the inside front or back of the card is lined. When lining the inside front of a card that has a window, you'll need to spray the card, not the paper—be sure to protect the areas (such as the card back) that shouldn't be sprayed.

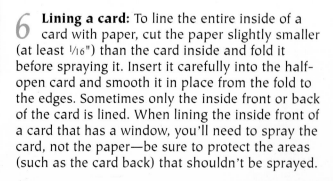

Making Envelopes

Make color-coordinated envelopes for your cards, or create custom envelopes for odd-sized cards. Envelopes which will be hand-delivered can be as bright and colorful as you want; it's fun to embellish them with bows, charms and stickers. An envelope which will go into the mail needs to meet postal rules for size. It should have a clear address area, and any embellishments must be flat and firmly attached.

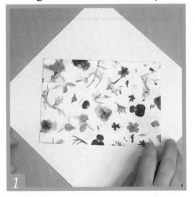

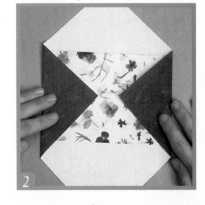

1 You'll need a perfect square of paper, at least 2" wider than the largest dimension of your card. Place the paper diagonally, front side down, with the card in the center as shown.

2 Holding the card firmly in place, fold in the two sides of the envelope, creasing the paper next to the card sides.

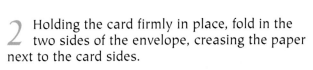

3 Fold the bottom flap up, again creasing the envelope next to the card edge. You'll be folding up part of the folded sides—this strengthens the corners (and if you want to add a spoonful of confetti for a fun touch, it will hold it in!).

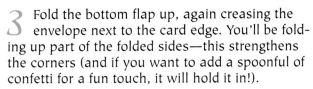

4 Repeat to fold the top flap down over the bottom flap—again, you'll fold in part of the sides.

5 Lift the top flap. Pull the bottom flap away from the sides, then apply a thin line of glue near the lower edge of each side flap. Press the bottom flap over the glue and hold for a moment to allow it to set.

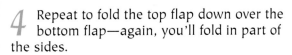

6 Use glue on the top flap edges, fold the flap down and hold while the glue sets. (*Optional:* Seal the top flap with a sticker, glued-on embellishment or a wax seal.)

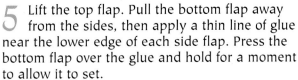

Jacie Pete
1250 NW 3rd
Canby OR 97013

Pocket Cards
by Marilyn Gossett

Balloon Card in Gift Pocket

papers: one 8½" square of blue candle-print paper, one 3½"x4" piece of purple paper with multi-colored dots (Paper Pizazz™ Birthday)
one 4½"x6¼" happy birthday card (Cards with Pizazz)
3 balloons cutout, 3 gifts cutout (Paper Pizazz™ Birthday)
decorative scissors (bow tie by Fiskars®)
black fine-tip pen, glue (see page 8)

1 Card: Glue the balloons to the dotted paper, then use the decorative scissors to cut ¼" away. Glue to the card front so the upper balloon extends 1" above the edge. Use the pen to draw balloon strings.

2 Pocket: Follow the diagram to crease the candle paper. Cut 1" in on each side where marked. Fold the top down, the sides in, then the bottom up. Tuck the bottom point inside. Glue the gifts to the envelope center, extending slightly above the opening edge. Insert the card into the envelope.

(diagram labels: 3¼", 5¼", 1½", 3⅝", 1", 1", 2⅜")

Bee Happy

blue clouds paper: one 8½" square, one 2"x5½" strip (Paper Pizazz™ Vacation)
one 8½"x5½" piece of bear & bees paper (Paper Pizazz™ Childhood)
one 2¾"x2" piece of white paper
two 10" long strands of raffia
1/16" thick wood pieces: two 1⅛" wide hearts, two 7/16" circles, two 1" long teardrops
acrylic paints: black, yellow; #3 round paintbrush
decorative scissors (jumbo wave by Family Treasures)
tracing paper, pencil, black fine-tip pen, glue (see page 8)

A card made from folded paper is trimmed with a strip to match the pocket. A white paper cloud, honeybees assembled from wood cutouts and a raffia shoestring bow embellish both pieces and tie them together.

Congratulations!

papers: one 8½"x11" sheet of pastel plaid, one 2"x2¼" piece of pastel plaid (Paper Pizazz™ Papers for Cards & Envelopes), one 9"x11" sheet of pink dotted (Paper Pizazz™ Light Great Backgrounds), one 11"x6" piece of white paper
1 lamb (Baby Punch-Outs™)
16" of gold elastic cord, black fine-tip pen
two 1" long silver safety pins
7" of ¼" wide mint satin ribbon
decorative scissors (jumbo wave by Family Treasures)

Cute as a lamb and easy to make, this card is just a piece of paper folded in fourths. An edged sheet of white paper was tied inside for a writing surface. The torn paper patch in the center matches the pocket and frames pins "hanging" from a satin bow.

"Buttons"

papers: one 8½" square of dog bones, one 8½"x5½" piece of paw prints (Paper Pizazz™ Pets), one 8½"x5½" piece of tan parchment, one 2"x2½" piece of blue
1 doghouse cutout (Paper Pizazz™ Pets)
small photo of pet (to fit on blue paper)
four 20" long strands of pink raffia
1 green bone-shaped dog biscuit
black fine-tip pen, glue (see page 8)

Put your pet in the doghouse! The photo was trimmed close to the dog, then matted on blue paper to fit inside the doghouse. The simple folded paper card is lined with parchment. A pocket (see page 16, step 2) of dog bones paper embellished with a real dog treat makes this card fun to receive for pet or person!

Hungry Frog

one 8½" square of ferns paper (Paper Pizazz™ Great Outdoors)
one 4½"x6¼" barnwood card (Cards with Pizazz)
1 flower cutout (Paper Pizazz™ Embellishments)
1 frog (Childhood Punch-Outs™)
four 14" long strands of raffia
one ½" wide plastic ladybug
one ⅜" thick foam mounting tape dot
Dimensional Magic™ (Plaid Enterprises, Inc.)
#4 flat paintbrush
glue (see page 8)

A pocket (see page 16, step 2) made of ferns paper is home to a threatened ladybug, while the frog is preparing to jump off the top right front of the card. Depth was created by mounting the frog on a foam dot. Glossy sealer adds a "wet look" to the frog and a gleam to the ladybug's wings.

Quilt Card

papers: one 8½" square of oatmeal handmade-look (Paper Pizazz™ Solid Muted Tones), one 8½"x11" sheet of Irish chain quilt (Paper Pizazz™ Country), one 9"x6" piece of mauve handmade-look (Paper Pizazz™ Handmade Papers)
two ⅝" wide pink buttons, one ⅝" wide green button
three 24" long strands of raffia
brass charms: one 1" long scissors, one ½" wide thimble
decorative scissors (pinking by Family Treasures)
black fine-tip pen, glue (see page 8)

Delight a seamstress' heart with a card made by folding a sheet of quilt-look paper in fourths. It's lined with mauve paper cut slightly larger so the decorative edges peek past the card. The pocket (see page 16, step 2) is made of a neutral paper. Both card and pocket are decorated with raffia bows and sewing items.

Shaker Box Cards

by Marilyn Gossett

See page 134 for helpful information on cutting windows.

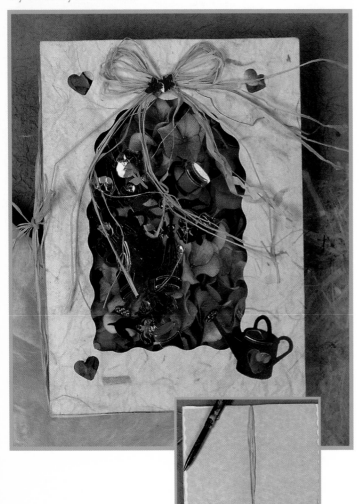

Hydrangea Garden Card

one 4½"x6¼" purple hydrangeas card (Cards with Pizazz)
papers: one 5"x6¾" piece of tan handmade-look (Paper
     Pizazz™ Handmade Papers), one 2" square of hydrangeas
     (Paper Pizazz™ Pretty Papers), two 9"x6¼" pieces of tan
     parchment
one 4½"x6¼" piece of foam board
one 4½"x6¼" piece of clear acetate
decorative scissors (jumbo wave by Family Treasures)
½" heart punch (Family Treasures)
"gardening" metallic confetti
½ oz. of raffia
4" tall arch template, craft knife, cutting mat, pencil
stylus or embossing tool, ruler
double-stick tape or glue (see page 8)

1 Trace the arch in the center of the foam board and
  onto the back center of the handmade-look paper.
Use the craft knife to cut out the foam board; glue the
acetate over the front. Use the decorative scissors to cut
⅛" inside the traced arch on the paper.

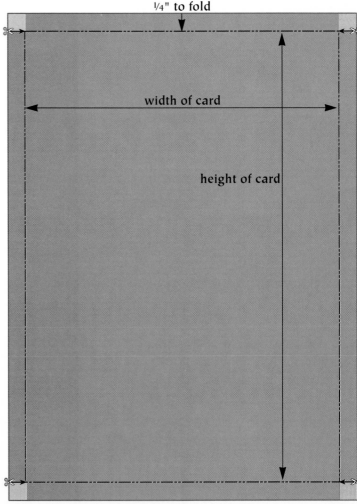

2 Measure and mark a line ¼" inside each edge of the
  paper. Cut just to the folds as indicated on the diagram. Fold on the dashed lines. Lay the paper, front side
up, on the foam board. Glue in place, overlapping the
flaps. Select a watering can and two small butterflies
from the confetti and set aside for step 3. Place the
remaining confetti in the window. Glue the front of the
card to the back of the foam board.

3 Cut eight 23" raffia lengths. Hold together and tie in
  a shoestring bow with 1" loops and 4½" tails. Glue
above the arch. Glue the confetti butterflies to the center
of the bow. Glue the watering can to the lower right corner of the arch. Punch four hearts from hydrangeas
paper. Glue one to the watering can and one to each
remaining corner of the arch.

4 Fold the parchment paper in half, then trim the 6¼"
  edges with the decorative scissors. Place one inside
the other, then place both inside the card. Cut four 13"
raffia lengths and tie them around all the folds to secure
the paper inside the card.

Christmas Plaid Card

one 4½"x6¼" pine boughs card (Cards with Pizazz)
one 5"x6¾" piece of Christmas plaid paper (Paper Pizazz™ Ho Ho Ho!!!)
one 4½"x6¼" piece of foam board, one 4½"x6¼" piece of clear acetate
decorative scissors (bow tie by Fiskars®)
Christmas metallic confetti, 1 tsp. of iridescent clear glitter
four 26" long strands of raffia
2¾"x4" oval template, craft knife, cutting mat, pencil
stylus or embossing tool, ruler, double-stick tape or glue (see page 8)

Adding glitter to the confetti inside the window gives a holiday card festive sparkle. The raffia bow is decorated with confetti trees.

"It's a Boy!" Card

one 6¼"x4½" rainbow hearts card (Cards with Pizazz)
one 6¾"x5" piece of baby blocks paper (Paper Pizazz™ Baby)
1 bunny, 1 "It's a Boy!" (Baby Punch-Outs™)
one 6¼"x4½" piece of foam board
one 6¼"x4½" piece of clear acetate
decorative scissors (Victorian by Fiskars®)
pink and blue baby bottles confetti
3¾" wide heart template, craft knife, cutting mat
pencil, stylus or embossing tool, ruler, double-stick tape or glue (see page 8)

A horizontal card made like the one on page 18 features a heart-shaped window and baby-themed embellishments. The bunny's ears extend above the fold line of the card for a charming, inquisitive touch.

Gold Crinkle Card
by Anne-Marie Spencer

one 4½"x6¼" gold swirl card (Cards with Pizazz)
papers: one 8½"x11" piece of brown suede-look (Paper Pizazz™ Black & White Photos), one 8½" square of metallic copper (Paper Pizazz™ Metallic Papers)
copper acrylic paint, makeup sponge
tracing paper, pencil, ruler
glue (see page 8)

1 Cut an 8½"x5½" piece of brown paper and crumple it tightly on a flat surface, then use the sponge to lightly dab copper paint onto the raised surfaces. Let dry. Slightly uncrinkle the paper and trim to 3½"x4¼". Glue the crinkled paper to the copper paper and trim ⅛" away on all sides. Repeat with brown paper.

2 Cut a 4½"x6¼" diamond from the remaining copper paper, then glue to the remaining brown paper and trim 1/16" away. Glue the diamond to the center of the card, then glue the rectangle over it as shown.

3-D Cards

by LeNae Gerig

Self-adhesive foam mounting tape or dots can be used to raise card elements to create a three-dimensional effect. They are available in different thicknesses, or they can be layered to create different heights.

"Welcome Home" Card

6¼"x4½" barnwood card (Cards with Pizazz)
papers: 5½"x3⅞" piece of green checked,
    (Paper Pizazz™ Dots, Checks, Plaids &
    Stripes), 4"x3" piece of green
1 apple (School Days Punch-Outs™)
4" tall oval template, pencil
black fine-tip pen
two ½" wide self-adhesive foam mounting dots
glue (see page 8)

1 Glue the checked paper to the center front of the card. Use the template to cut a green oval and glue to the center of the checked paper.

2 Write "Welcome Home" in the center of the green oval. Draw a border of squiggles and dots around the oval; repeat around the outside of the card front.

3 Affix one foam dot to the top of the apple and the other near the bottom. Adhere the apple at the lower right as shown, overlapping the oval.

Trick-or-Treat Card & Envelope

one 9"x6¼" piece of blue cardstock
papers: one 3⅞"x5⅜" piece of blue stars paper (Paper Pizazz™ Adult Birthday), one 8½" square of candy corn paper (Paper Pizazz™ Holidays & Seasons), one 4"x5½" piece of black, one 4"x4½" piece of black, one 1¼"x2" piece of black
Halloween stickers: one 3¾" tall witch, one 1¾" tall cat, seven assorted ½" long candies (Provo Craft®)
decorative scissors (spindle by Fiskars®)
six ½" wide self-adhesive foam mounting dots
ruler, stylus or embossing tool, glue (see page 8)

1 **Card:** Make a card from the cardstock (see page 14). Glue the 4"x5½" piece of black paper to the center front. Trim the stars paper with the decorative scissors, then glue to the center of the black paper.

2 Adhere the witch and cat stickers to the remaining pieces of black paper, then use straight scissors to trim ⅛" away. Use four foam dots to mount the witch in the card center. Mount the cat as shown.

3 **Envelope:** Use the candy corn paper to make an envelope for the card (see page 15). Use the decorative scissors to trim the flap.

Cutaway Card

by LeNae Gerig

one 4¹⁄₂"x6¹⁄₄" pine boughs card (Cards with Pizazz)
1 elf ornament (Christmas Punch-Outs™)
papers: one 4¹⁄₂"x6¹⁄₄" piece of red, one 1¹⁄₈"x6¹⁄₄" piece of
*   green, one ⁷⁄₈"x6¹⁄₄" piece of yellow*
decorative scissors (ripply by McGill, Inc.)
glue (see page 8)

Line the inside back of the card with the red paper (see page 14). Use the decorative scissors to trim 2" off the right edge of the card front. Glue the yellow strip behind the front and trim ¹⁄₄" away, matching the pattern of the front. Repeat with the green strip. Glue the Punch-Out™ centered on the exposed edges.

Bi-Fold Ballerina Card

by LeNae Gerig

one 9"x6¹⁄₄" piece of blue cardstock
papers: 1³⁄₄"x6¹⁄₄" piece of pink/blue plaid (Paper Pizazz™
*   Light Great Backgrounds), one 8¹⁄₂" square of ballerina*
*   hearts (Paper Pizazz™ Little Charmers)*
1 ballerina (Punch-Outs™ for Cards)
yellow paper: one 1⁷⁄₈"x6¹⁄₄" piece, one 4"x4¹⁄₂" piece
³⁄₄" tall pink sticker letters (Déjà Views)
white opaque pen (Zig®)
decorative scissors (ripple by Fiskars®)
ruler, stylus or embossing tool, glue (see page 8)

1 **Card:** Make a card from the cardstock (see page 14). Trim both edges of the plaid strip with the decorative scissors; glue it to the center of the yellow strip. Glue to the inside back, ¹⁄₄" from the edge. Score and fold half of the front back. Glue the ballerina to the 4" piece of yellow paper, trim ¹⁄₈" away and glue overlapping the fold as shown. Use the white pen to draw random stars and dots over the front fold. Use stickers to write the recipient's name.

2 **Envelope:** Use the ballerina paper to make an envelope for the card (see page 15). Use the decorative scissors to trim the envelope flap.

It's a Boy!

SUPER BOWL PARTY

10   40

A Birthday Surprise

It's A Girl!!

Ice Cream Party

OPEN HOUSE please come!

OCT 19

Invitations & Announcements

We find all types of occassions to announce an event throughout our lives: the birth of a baby, the engagement of a friend, the wedding of a son and the graduation of a daughter are all milestones we want to share with friends and loved ones. The same is true of invitations. We throw all sorts of parties for all sorts of reasons; sending out invitations is just the beginning of all the fun to come.

This chapter will show you techniques for making your own invitations at a fraction of the cost of store-bought ones. Simple patterns or die cuts can be cut to make a card in almost any shape. Mount it on patterned paper and cardstock and you have a terrific invitation or announcement. For those very special occasions, a bit of laser-cut lace paper or a few ribbon roses make your invitation or announcement as elegant as the event itself.

Scissors, glue and paper are the basic tools needed to create these designs. But you'll also find uses for punches, stickers and die-cut patterns. Embellishments, such as buttons, ribbon or a few ribbon flowers, can be glued or tied on to add your own personal touch. Using the ideas in this chapter, you'll find that sending out invitations and announcements has never been so much fun!

Cards with Die Cuts

by LeNae Gerig

Die cuts are marvelous when you need to make dozens of invitations or announcements. Shapes can be cut in one stroke, and several thicknesses of paper can be cut at once.

To cut a folded shape, fold the paper or cardstock before inserting it into the machine. Be sure the folded edge is inside the die where you want it to be uncut.

If you don't have access to a die-cut machine, use the pattern provided and cut the shape with scissors or a craft knife. Just be sure to leave a section of the fold intact.

Balloon Birthday Invitation

papers: one 5"x4½" piece of balloons on white, one 5½"x5" piece of red checked (Paper Patch®)
cardstock: one 5¾"x5½" piece of yellow, one 8"x6" piece of red
balloon die (Accu/Cut® Systems)
black broad-tip pen, glue (see page 8)

Glue the balloon paper to the checked paper, then glue the checked paper to the yellow cardstock. Fold the red card stock in half, place the fold inside the balloon die and cut. Write "A Birthday Surprise" on the front of the balloon. Glue to the invitation front. Open the card and give party details on the inside.

© & ™ Accu/Cut® Systems, Inc.

Super Bowl Party

papers: one 4⅞"x4½" piece of football field, one 5⅝"x5¼" piece of footballs (Paper Pizazz™ Sports), one 1" square of white
cardstock: one 5⅞"x5½" piece of green, one 9"x4" piece of blue
football helmet die (Accu/Cut® Systems)
1" wide star punch (Family Treasures)
pens: black, metallic gold
glue (see page 8)

© & ™ Accu/Cut® Systems, Inc.

Glue the footballs paper to the green cardstock and the field paper to the footballs paper. Fold the blue cardstock in half, place the fold inside the helmet die and cut. Punch a white star and glue it to the right helmet; make a gold dot in each point of the star. Write "SUPER BOWL PARTY" on the front of the helmet and the party details inside. Glue the helmet to the card front.

Tip: Cut the helmet in your team colors, and choose a punch to match its logo.

Open House

papers: one 5"x4½" piece of apple print, one 5½"x5" piece
of red and green plaid (Paper Patch®)
cardstock: one 8"x4½" piece of red, one 5¾"x5½" piece of
green, one 1"x1½" piece of green
apple die (Accu/Cut® Systems)
black fine-tip pen, glue (see page 8)

Glue the apple paper to the checked paper, then glue the
checked paper to the large piece of green cardstock. Fold
the red card stock in half, place the fold inside the apple
die and cut. Use just the leaf area of the die to cut a green
leaf; glue to the apple. Write "OPEN HOUSE Please
come!" on the front of the balloon and the date, time etc.
inside. Glue to the invitation front.

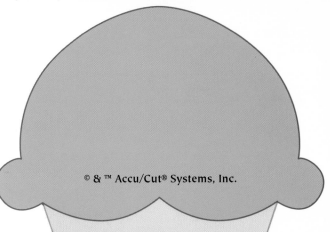

Ice Cream Party

papers: one 5"x4½" piece of rainbow sweets (Paper Pizazz™
Childhood), one 5½"x5" piece of peach with pastel dots
(Paper Pizazz™ Light Great Backgrounds)
cardstock: one 5¾"x5¼" piece of aqua, one 4"x2½" piece
of aqua, one 6"x4½" piece of light brown
ice cream cone die (Accu/Cut® Systems)
fine-tip pens: black, purple
ruler, glue (see page 8)

Glue the sweets paper to the pastel paper, then glue the
pastel paper to the large piece of aqua cardstock. Fold
the brown card stock in half, place the fold inside the
cone area of the die and cut. Use the black pen and
ruler to draw waffle lines on the cone. Use the scoop
area of the die to cut an aqua scoop; glue to the cone
top. Write "Ice Cream Party" on the scoop and the party
details inside the cone. Glue to the invitation front.

Graduation Party

one 5"x4½" piece of graduation paper (Paper Pizazz™ School Days)

cardstock: one 5¾"x5¼" piece of red, one 6"x5½" piece of black, one 4½"x7" piece of black

fine-tip pens: black, white, metallic gold

mortarboard die (Accu/Cut® Systems)

glue (see page 8)

Glue the graduation paper to the red cardstock, then glue the red cardstock to the large piece of black cardstock. Fold the small piece of black cardstock in half, place the fold inside the mortarboard die and cut. Use the black pen to write "Class of '98" repeatedly around the edge of the card base, separated with gold dots. Use the white pen to write "Graduation Party" on the mortarboard and glue it to the card front. Write the party details inside the mortarboard with the white pen.

Tip: Use your school colors for the cardstock.

© & ™ Accu/Cut® Systems, Inc.

Baby Announcement

papers: one 4⅝"x5" piece of pink baby bottle print, one 5⅛"x5¾" piece of pink/white plaid, one 3"x1½" piece of pink/white plaid (Paper Patch®)

white cardstock: one 6"x5¼" piece, one 5⅜"x6" piece

9" of ⅝" wide pink satin ribbon

baby bottle die (Accu/Cut® Systems)

purple calligraphy pen, glue (see page 8)

Glue the bottles paper to the 5" piece of plaid paper, then glue the plaid paper to the large piece of white cardstock. Fold the remaining cardstock in half, place the remaining plaid strip across the center, place the fold inside the bottle die and cut. Write "Baby" on the front of the bottle and the baby details inside. Glue to the announcement front. Use the ribbon to make a shoestring bow with 1" loops and 1½" tails; glue to the bottle neck.

Tip: Change the colors to suit a "boy" announcement or a baby shower.

It's a Girl!

by Marilyn Gossett

*papers: one 12" square of pink tri-dots, one
8½"x6¾" piece of pink tri-dots (Paper
Pizazz™ Baby's First Year), one 8"x6" piece
of "It's a Girl!", one 3½"x6" piece of "It's a
Girl!" (Paper Pizazz™ Baby)*
1 baby girl bear (Baby Punch-Outs™)
one ¾" wide wood heart button
acrylic paints: pink, white
#4 flat paintbrush
black fine-tip pen
Dimensional Magic™ (Plaid Enterprises, Inc.)
*decorative scissors (bow tie by Fiskars®, wave
by Family Treasures)*
glue (see page 8)

1 Fold the 8½" piece of pink paper in half,
then trim with the bow tie scissors. Write
the details of the announcement on the inside
back. Fold the 8" piece of "It's a Girl!" in half
and insert the pink paper inside. Follow the
diagram to fold the 12" square of pink paper
into an envelope, then insert the card into it.

2 Follow the instructions for the Triple-Fold
Tags on page 52 to make a tag from the
small piece of "It's a Girl!" paper. Use the
decorative scissors to trim the long edges and
the flap. Glue it to the envelope front with the
bear "sitting" on it as shown.

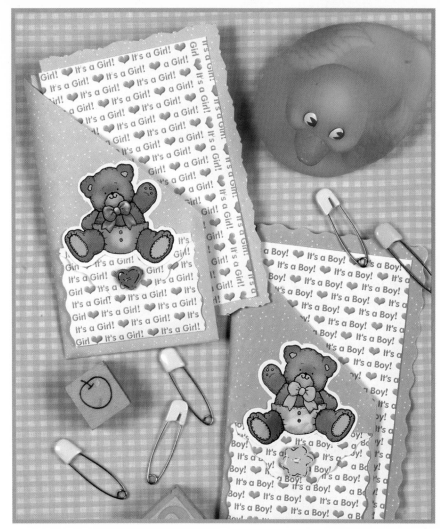

3 Paint the button pink; let dry. Paint a white "stitch" between the
holes. Use the pen to embellish the edges with a — • — border and
draw a dash in the center of the stitch. Follow the manufacturer's instructions to apply Dimensional Magic™ to the button; let dry. Glue the button
to the tag flap below the bear.

It's a Boy!

by Marilyn Gossett

*papers: one 12" square of blue tri-dots, one 8½"x6¾"
piece of blue tri-dots (Paper Pizazz™ Baby's First Year),
one 8"x6" piece of "It's a Boy!", one 3½"x6" piece of
"It's a Boy!" (Paper Pizazz™ Baby)*
1 baby boy bear (Baby Punch-Outs™)
one ¾" wide wood flower button
acrylic paints: yellow, white
#4 flat paintbrush, black fine-tip pen
Dimensional Magic™ (Plaid Enterprises, Inc.)
decorative scissors (wave by Family Treasures)
glue (see page 8)

Make as for the "It's a Girl!" card, using the listed
papers and materials.

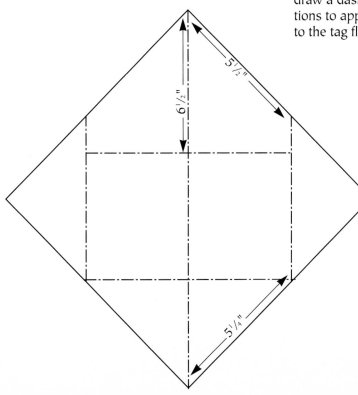

Lacy Formals
by Eunice Sherwood

Laser-printed Invitation:

one 3³⁄₄"x8¹⁄₂" piece of laser lace (Paper Pizazz™ Romantic Papers)
one 4"x8³⁄₄" piece of white card-stock
4¹⁄₈" length of ¹⁄₄" wide white satin ribbon
¹⁄₄" hole punch
color laser or inkjet printer

Hand-lettered Invitation:

one 5"x8" piece of laser lace (Paper Pizazz™ Romantic Papers)
one 5¹⁄₂"x8¹⁄₂" piece of silver cardstock
4¹⁄₈" length of ³⁄₈" wide silver/gold woven ribbon
¹⁄₄" hole punch, black and gold calligraphy pens, black fine-tip pen

1 **Printed invitation:** Print your invitation in the plain area of the lace paper so the lace is at the top (you should be able to print three invitations side by side). Center the lace on the cardstock, then punch holes ⁵⁄₈" apart at the top center. Insert the ribbon through the holes, front to back, then bring each end back up through the opposite hole.

2 **Hand-lettered invitation:** Letter in the plain area of the lace. Assemble as for the printed invitation in step 1.

Lacy Heart Engagement Card

by LeNae Gerig

one 4¹⁄₂"x6¹⁄₄" brown swirl card (Cards with Pizazz)
one 4"x3" piece of laser lace paper (Paper Pizazz™ Romantic Papers)
one 4"x5" piece of brown paper
9" of ¹⁄₈" wide ivory satin ribbon
decorative scissors (Victorian by Fiskars®)
tracing paper, pencil, glue (see page 8)

1 Trace the heart pattern, then place one straight edge (shown as a blue dotted line) on the fold of the card and trace the heart onto the card. Cut out.

2 Use the same pattern to cut the shoulders of the heart from the laser lace; glue to the card. Glue the folded card to the brown paper, then trim ¹⁄₈" away with decorative scissors.

3 Use the ribbon to make a shoestring bow with ³⁄₄" loops and 2" tails. Glue to the top point of the heart. Write your announcement inside the card.

Announcement with Lace Envelope

by LeNae Gerig

one 4¹/₂"x6¹/₄" pastel quilt card (Cards with Pizazz)
³/₈" wide ribbon roses with green leaves: 1 blue, 1 pink
12" of ¹/₄" wide blue satin ribbon
one 4" wide white round paper doily
one 8" white square paper doily
decorative scissors (mini antique by Family Treasures)
magenta fine-tip pen, glue (see page 8)

Cut the card to a 4¹/₂" square, then trim the right opening edges with the decorative scissors. Glue the round doily to the card center and write "It's a Girl!" on it. Use the ribbon to make a shoestring bow with 1" loops and 4" tails; glue to the doily as shown. Glue the pink rose to the bow center. Place the square doily diagonally on the table with the card in the center. Fold the right and left doily corners over the card—they should overlap slightly. Fold the bottom corner up and glue to secure. Glue the blue rose to the top point of the bottom flap.

Pop-Up Party Card

by LeNae Gerig

one 6¹/₄"x4¹/₂" Christmas candies card (Cards with Pizazz)
postcard, elf (Punch-Outs™ for Cards), "Good Boys & Girls List" (Pop-Ups for Cards)
4¹/₂"x3¹/₄" piece of red/green/white striped paper (Paper Pizazz™ Christmas)
4³/₄"x3¹/₂" piece of red paper
1"x4" strip of white paper
decorative scissors (ripply by McGill, Inc.)
black fine-tip pen, glue (see page 8)

1 **Card front:** Use the decorative scissors to trim the card end. Trim the edges of the striped paper, glue it to the red paper, then trim ¹/₈" away. Glue to the center front of the card. Glue the postcard and elf as shown. Use the pen to write "All I WANT FOR CHRISTMAS IS TO GO TO the (YOUR NAME)'S PARTY!"

2 **Inside:** Write the details of your invitation on the Christmas list. Fold the 1"x4" strip in fourths as shown in the diagram. Glue the bottom to the inside back, close to the fold. Glue the top to the inside front, 1" above the fold. Glue the list to the vertical area.

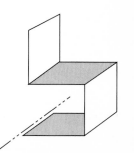

1 black haunted house die cut (Accu/Cut® Systems)
papers: one 7"x9³/₄" piece of gray, one 1¹/₄"x1³/₄" piece of gray, one ¹/₂" circle of gray, one 5¹/₂"x8¹/₂" piece of yellow, one 2"x⁵/₈" piece of black, two ³/₄"x1³/₄" pieces of light brown, one ³/₈"x⁵/₈" piece of blue, one ³/₄" square of dark gray
pens: black broad-tip, black fine-tip, metallic gold, orange, white
Halloween stickers (©Mrs. Grossman's Paper Co.)

1 Cut the large piece of gray paper slightly larger than the die cut, varying the width for an irregular look. Glue the edges of the die cut to the gray paper. Use the pattern to cut the yellow paper, then slip it between the gray paper and the die cut to make sure it fits; trim if necessary.

2 Use the black pen to write the details of your invitation on areas of the yellow paper which will be covered by the die cut. Place stickers in the areas which will show through the windows. Write "Open at your own risk" inside the door area. Glue the small piece of black to the yellow paper below the door as a pull tab.

3 Embellish the house with stickers as shown. Use the gold pen to draw a door frame, bricks on the chimney and windowsills. Write "Costume Party" above the front door. Draw gold "eyes" and squiggles scattered across the front.

4 Cut the small pieces of brown and gray paper into tombstones—use the patterns given or create your own styles! Embellish with the fine point pen and glue as shown.

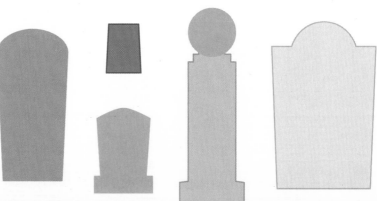

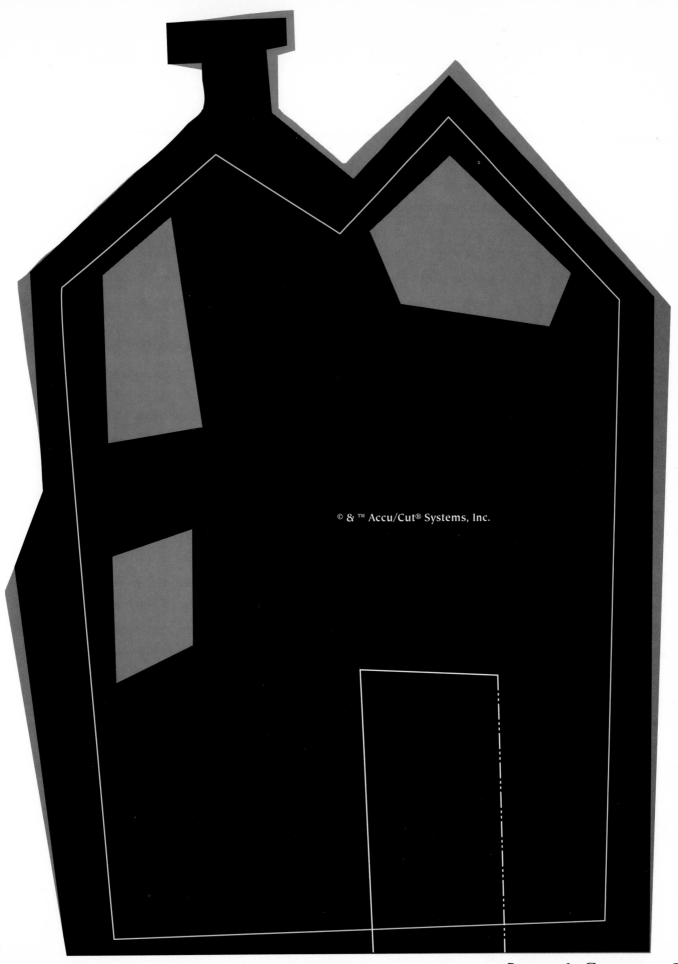

© & ™ Accu/Cut® Systems, Inc.

A friend
is a present
you give yourself.

It's in the Bag

Gift bags are a simple and easy alternative to gift-wrapping. With a little tissue paper to cover the top, they're as much fun to open as a wrapped present—even for kids!

This chapter shows you how to make gift bags of any size. After you learn the basic techniques, you can tailor your bag to the size of your gift, or make one to fit a special gift-giving occasion.

The bags in this chapter are made from as little as half a sheet of paper or a standard card, to as much as two store-bought gift bags that are cut apart and glued to make a one-of-a-kind design! Plain or patterned papers, ribbon, yarn, buttons and other tidbits can be turned into adorable faces, hair and bow ties to make some very cute gift-bag characters. Patterned or plain papers can be punched, edged, rounded, stamped or drawn upon to embellish small bags. And charms or flower buds add a touch of elegance to these bags!

Once you've finished reading this chapter, your biggest problem will be figuring out what to put inside these terrific little bags.

Mini Gift Bags

by Marilyn Gossett

Fun to make from cardstock or paper, these small bags are perfect for jewelry or other small gifts. The construction is easily adaptable to smaller or larger bags.

for each bag:
pencil, ruler, stylus or embossing tool
glue (see page 8), 1/4" hole punch

Refer to the diagram on page 35. Use the ruler and stylus to score the wrong side of the cardstock or paper along the fold lines (be careful when scoring lightweight paper, as it may tear with too much pressure). Cut to each vertical line as shown. Crease on all scored lines. Fold along the scored lines, overlapping 1/2" in back, and glue the seam together. Fold the bottom side flaps in, the back flap forward and the front flap backward; glue to secure. Punch a hole in each side, 1/2" below the top edge. Insert one handle end through each hole, outside to inside. Knot or glue to secure. Embellish as shown in the photos.

Burgundy Bag

one 9 1/2"x4 1/4" piece of burgundy cardstock
decorative scissors (wave by Family Treasures)
9" of pearlescent wired paper twist
six 18" long strands of raffia
two 1" sprigs of mauve silk baby's breath
three 1/2" wide white silk forget-me-nots
one 1 1/2" long sprig of artificial lavender with three 1" long blossom spikes
one 1" long green silk rose leaf

Trim the decorative edge on the top before folding.

Blue Corrugated Bag

papers: one 9 1/2"x4 1/4" piece of blue corrugated-look (Paper Pizazz™ Country), one 2 1/4"x2 3/4" piece of beige handmade-look (Paper Pizazz™ Handmade Papers), one 1 5/8"x2 1/4" piece of pink hydrangeas (Paper Pizazz™ Pretty Papers)
decorative scissors (wave by Family Treasures, pinking by Fiskars®)
raffia: three 18" long strands, three 36" long strands
one 1/2" wide mauve ribbon rose with green ribbon leaves
one 1" wide brass basket charm

The handle was braided from 36" strands of raffia. Edged panels on the front pick up the rose and raffia colors.

Ivory Sachet Bag

one 9 1/2"x4 1/4" piece of ivory cardstock
9" of white wired paper twist
one 4" round white paper doily
four 12" long strands of raffia
12" of 6" wide white tulle net, 2 Tbsp. of potpourri
one 1" long pink paper rosebud
four 1/2" long yellow paper rosebuds

Floral Paper Bag

one 9 1/2"x4 1/4" piece of handmade-look paper with pink and purple flowers (Paper Pizazz™ Handmade Papers)
decorative scissors (pinking by Fiskars®)
1 yard of 1/8" wide pink satin ribbon
1 yard of 1/4" wide metallic gold ribbon
one 1/2" wide pink ribbon rose with green ribbon leaves

Multiple ribbons give a delicate, rich look to a printed bag.

three 3/4" long green silk rose leaves
three 1" long sprigs of white silk baby's breath

To make the sachet insert: Cut a 6" piece of tulle. Place the potpourri in the center and gather the tulle around it; tie with raffia. Gather the remaining tulle around the flowers to make the center bouquet.

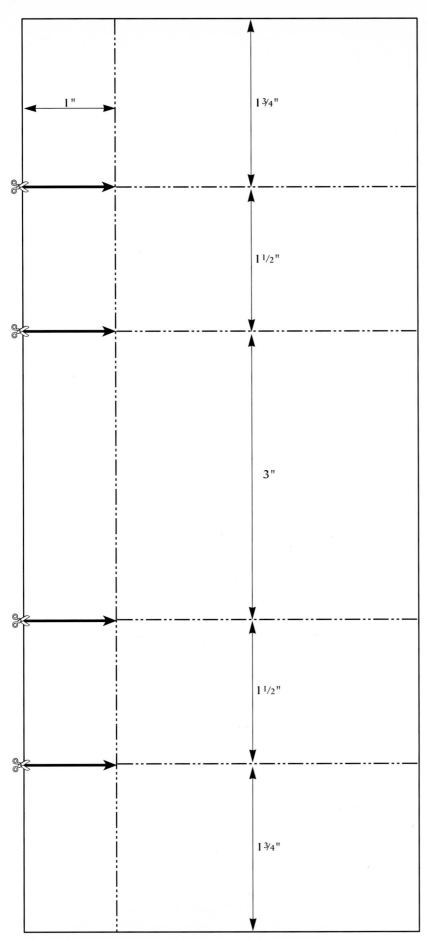

1"

1 ¾"

1 ½"

3"

1 ½"

1 ¾"

Dogwood Bag

one 9½"x4¼" piece of ivory cardstock
1 yard of 6" wide white tulle
one 2½" wide ivory silk dogwood blossom
*   with leaves*
two 1" long sprigs of white silk baby's breath
7" of white wired paper twist

To make a puffier bow, cut the ribbon (here, tulle) in half and hold the lengths together to tie the bow. You'll get double loops and tails.

Roses & Raffia Bag

one 9½"x4¼" piece of ivory handmade
*   cardstock with wood chips*
7" of pink wired paper twist
two 18" long strands of raffia
one 1" long pink paper rosebud
three ½" long yellow paper rosebuds
three 1" long green silk leaves
two 1" long sprigs of white silk baby's breath

For a fluffier look, use your fingernail to shred the loops and tails of the raffia bow.

Ho Ho Ho Bag

papers: one 9½"x4¼" piece of dark green with white stars (Paper Pizazz™ Dots, Stripes, Checks & Plaids), one 1½"x3½" piece of red/white striped, one 1⅛"x2¼" piece of Ho Ho Ho (Paper Pizazz™ Ho Ho Ho!!!)
five 18" long strands of raffia
one ⅜" wide brass locked heart charm
9" of dark green wired paper twist
decorative scissors (pinking by Fiskars®)

Wired paper twist, available in a variety of colors and textures, works great for bag handles. Most of the time (unless your gift is heavy) it's not even necessary to glue it—just fold each end up ½" on the inside of the bag.

Plaid Bag With Lid

papers: one 9½"x4¼" piece of green tartan, one 2¼" square of Christmas plaid, one 4⅛"x2⅛" piece of gingerbread, one 1¾" square of gingerbread (Paper Pizazz™ Ho Ho Ho!!!)
buttons: one ¾" wide natural, one ½" wide red
four 36" long strands of raffia
decorative scissors (pinking by Fiskars®)

To make the lid: Cut a ½" notch out of each corner of the 4⅛" gingerbread piece. Fold the edges down ½" and trim with the decorative scissors. Glue the back flap inside the top back edge of the box. Glue the buttons to the lid front. Edge the remaining paper pieces and glue to the front as shown. Tie the box shut with the raffia, making a shoestring bow with 1½" loops and 6" tails.

Pleated Gift Folders

by Marilyn Gossett

Paper folders, pleated for extra room, make great presentation envelopes for gifts of money or small items. Make one in any size you need, or use leftover papers to make bags to save for special occasions.

Basic instructions: Refer to the diagram on page 39. Fold under ¼" on each long side of the paper. Decide if you want a flap, and how deep (the one on the pink folder at right is 1"), then fold the flap down. Turn the paper wrong side up and fold the bottom short edge up to meet the flap fold; crease the bottom fold. Open, turn over and fold up ¼" on each side of the bottom fold; crease. Glue the side edges together.

Pink Roses Folder

papers: one 4"x8" piece of pink roses, one 1"x4" piece of pink moiré (Paper Pizazz™ Wedding)
decorative scissors (deckle by Family Treasures)
3" of ⅛" wide green ribbon
glue (see page 8)

1   **To make the paper tassel:** Cut ¾" deep fringe ⅛" apart in the 1"x4" paper strip. Roll up tightly, gluing the uncut edge. Wrinkle and fluff the fringe.

2   Trim the flap with the decorative scissors. Tie the top of the tassel with the ribbon and glue to the flap center.

Christmas Folders

for each folder:
decorative scissors (pinking by Fiskars®)
four 18" long strands of raffia
glue (see page 8), 1/4" hole punch
plaid folder:
*papers: one 4"x10 1/4" piece of green
    and red plaid, one 2 3/8" square of
    Christmas plaid, one 1 3/4" square
    of gingerbread (Paper Pizazz™ Ho
    Ho Ho!!!)*
*buttons: one 3/4" wide tan, one 1/2"
    wide red bow*
gingerbread folder:
*papers: one 4"x9 1/4" piece of ginger-
    bread, one 2 1/8" square of red with
    white dots, one 1" square of green
    plaid (Paper Pizazz™ Ho Ho Ho!!!)*
one 3/4" wide red button
10" of 1/8" wide red satin ribbon

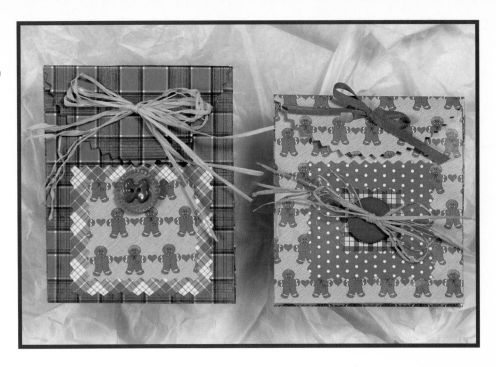

Follow the basic instructions on page 36 to make the folder. Use the decorative scissors to trim the flap and the paper squares. Glue the squares as shown. Punch two holes 1/2" apart 1/2" below the top folder edge. **Plaid folder:** Thread the raffia through the holes and tie in a shoestring bow with 1 1/2" loops and 3" tails. Glue the buttons below the flap as shown. **Gingerbread folder:** Thread the ribbon through the holes and tie in a shoestring bow with 3/4" loops and 1 1/2" tails. Thread the raffia through the buttonholes and tie in a shoestring bow with 1 1/4" loops and 2 1/2" tails. Glue the button to the center front.

Snowflake Envelopes

for each folder:
decorative scissors (wave by Family Treasures)
glue (see page 8), 1/4" hole punch
snowflakes folder:
*one 4 1/4"x10 1/2" piece of blue paper with snowflakes (Paper
    Pizazz™ Christmas)*
one 8" round white paper doily

1 yard of 1/8" blue satin ribbon
clear iridescent glitter
snowman folder:
*paper: one 4 1/4"x9 1/2" piece of blue with snowflakes (Paper
    Pizazz™ Christmas), one 1" square of yellow*
1 snowman (Christmas Punch-Outs™)
decorative scissors (bow tie by Fiskars®)
four 18" long strands raffia
*metallic confetti: one 3/4" tall green tree, 40–50 silver stars
    1/2" star punch (Family Treasures)*

Follow the basic instructions on page 36 to make each folder. Use the wave scissors to trim each flap. Punch two holes 1/2" apart 1/2" below each top folder edge. **Snowflakes:** Cut out "snowflakes" from the doily and glue to the envelope as shown. Apply glue and glitter to the snowflakes; shake off excess. Thread the ribbon through the holes and tie in a shoestring bow with 2" loops and 4" tails. **Snowman:** Thread the raffia through the holes and tie in a shoestring bow with 1 1/2" loops and 5" tails. Punch a star from yellow paper and glue to the bow center. Trim around the snowman with the bow tie scissors, then glue to the front of the folder. Glue the confetti as shown.

Birthday Folder

one 5"x10½" piece of party hats paper (Paper Pizazz™ Birthdays)
SURPRISE!!!, party hat, balloon (Celebrations Punch-Outs™)
plastic confetti: 1" wide Happy Birthday, two ¾" tall gifts
three 12" lengths of ¼" wide yellow curling ribbon
glue (see page 8)

Follow the basic instructions on page 36 to make the folder. Glue the SURPRISE!!! to the flap. Glue the balloon, hat and confetti to the front as shown. Knot the ribbon lengths together in the center, curl and shred. Glue the knot to the balloon string.

Hearts & Kisses

papers: one 5"x10½" piece of kisses (Paper Pizazz™ Teen Years), one 3½"
* square of tri-dots on pink (Paper Pizazz™ Light Great Backgrounds)*
"friends" heart (Sayings Punch-Outs™)
6" of metallic gold elastic thread, needle
one ½" wide brass heart charm
three 6" lengths of metallic gold shredded ribbon
decorative scissors (wave by Family Treasures)
glue (see page 8), one ⅜" wide double-stick foam dot

Follow the basic instructions on page 36 to make the folder. Glue the heart to the pink paper. Use the decorative scissors to trim ¼" away and to trim the flap. Tie the elastic thread to the charm. Use the needle to sew the thread ends through the heart as shown; knot in the back. Use the foam dot to attach the heart to the folder. Hold the shredded ribbon lengths together and tie a shoestring bow with 1" loops and 3" tails; glue to the flap.

Lacy Pleated Folder

papers: one 5"x10½" piece of antique lace (Paper Pizazz™ Black &
* White Photos), one 5"x2" piece of tri-dots on pink (Paper Pizazz™*
* Light Great Backgrounds), one 4"x3" piece of pink moiré (Paper*
* Pizazz™ Wedding), one 1"x2" piece of pink roses (Paper Pizazz™*
* Holidays & Seasons)*
two 12" lengths of ⅛" wide green satin ribbon
decorative scissors (wave by Family Treasures)
tracing paper, pencil, glue (see page 8), ¼" hole punch

Follow the basic instructions on page 36 to make the folder. Use decorative scissors to trim the flap, then glue the pink paper to the back of the flap and trim ¼" away. Punch two holes in the flap, ½" apart and ¼" below the top edge. Knot the ribbon lengths together at the center. Thread two ends through the punched holes and tie in back, making a shoestring bow with ¾" loops and 1" tails. Cut four large moiré hearts and two small rose hearts. Glue two moiré hearts wrong sides together, sandwiching the center of one ribbon tail 1" below the knot. Glue a rose heart to the front. Repeat with the other ribbon tail, but place this heart 2¼" below the knot.

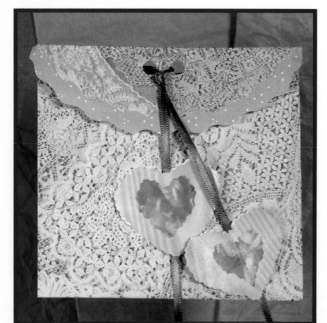

Floral Folder with "Lace" Trim

one 5"x10½" piece of floral handmade-look paper (Paper Pizazz™ Handmade Papers)
one 4" round white doily, 9" of ¼" wide metallic gold ribbon
decorative scissors (wave by Family Treasures)
¼" hole punch, glue (see page 8)

Follow the basic instructions on page 36 to make the folder. Use decorative scissors to trim the flap. Cut the doily in half and glue behind the flap to form a lace edging. Punch two holes in the flap, ½" apart and ¼" below the top edge. Thread the ribbon through the holes and tie in a shoestring bow with 1" loops and 1½" tails.

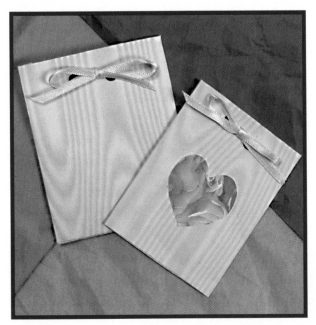

Flat Folders
by Marilyn Gossett

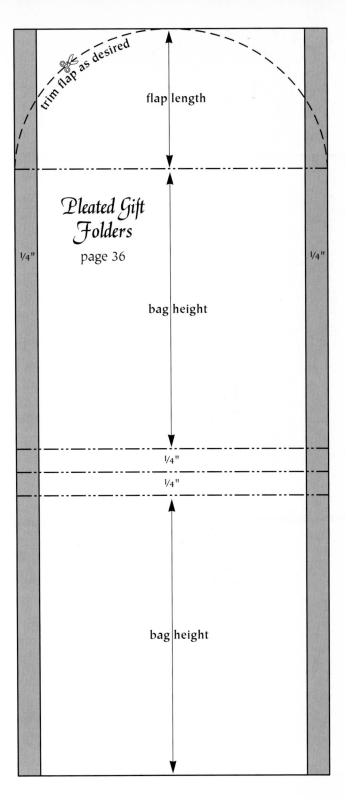

trim flap as desired

flap length

Pleated Gift Folders
page 36

¼"   ¼"

bag height

¼"
¼"

bag height

Basic instructions: Cut paper or lightweight cardstock to twice the desired width plus 1", and the desired height plus 1". Fold the top and bottom edges under ½". Overlap the back edges 1" and glue, then flatten the folder with the seam at the center back. Punch two holes ½" apart in the top and tie with ribbon.

for each folder shown:
10" of ⅛" wide pink satin ribbon, glue (see page 8), ¼" paper punch
gray folder: *one 6½"x4½" piece of white moiré paper (Paper Pizazz™)*
pink folder: *papers: one 6"x3¾" piece of pink moiré, 1 heart cut from a 1½" square of pink roses (Paper Pizazz™)*

Embellished Bags

by Tammi Schroeder

Plain gift bags are so much more economical than the printed ones from stationery stores—and just look what you can do with them!

"Bronze" Star Bag

one 7"x10"x4" brown paper bag with handles
six 12" long strands of raffia
one 4" square of white posterboard
white paint pen
acrylic paints: black, bronze
dimensional paint (any color), gloss acrylic varnish
1/2" flat paintbrush, paper towels, paper plate
tracing paper, transfer paper, pencil
glue (see page 8)

1 Trace the patterns. Transfer the zig-zag, serpentine and dashed line to the bag top, repeating as needed. Transfer the flower and spiral to the bag bottom, repeating as needed. Draw over the lines with the white pen.

2 Transfer the star pattern to the posterboard and cut out. Squeeze over the spiral and squiggle lines with dimensional paint; let dry. Paint the entire star with bronze paint; let dry. Mix black paint with an equal amount of water and brush onto the star. Dab off excess paint with a paper towel. Let dry, then varnish.

3 Hold the raffia together and form into 3" loop with 3" tails. Glue to the bag center. Glue the star to the raffia center.

Heart Friend Bag

acrylic paints: green, rust, dusty rose, lavender
black fine-tip pen
8"x4" piece of butcher paper, pencil, craft knife
paintbrushes: #1 liner, 1/2" stencil or deerfoot
18" of 3/8" wide pink satin ribbon
glue (see page 8)

Use the pen to write "A friend is a present you give yourself" on the bag center front. Referring to the photo for placement, trace the heart patterns onto butcher paper and carefully cut out the hearts to make a stencil. Hold the stencil in place on the bag front and stipple the hearts, varying the colors as shown. Discard the stencil and let the paint dry. Use the liner with green paint to stroke on grass blades. Use the ribbon to make a shoe-string bow with 2" loops and 4" tails; glue below the lettering.

Tuxedo Bag

one 7"x9"x4" glossy burgundy bag with handles
glossy paper: one 3"x8" piece of white, one 6"x8" piece of black
15" of 3" wide burgundy checked paper ribbon
black acrylic paint
#3 round paintbrush
glue (see page 8)

(The pattern is on page 142.) Glue triangles of black and white paper as shown to form the tuxedo lapels, then paint "buttons" down the front. Cut 3" of paper ribbon and set aside. Form the remaining ribbon into a bow shape and wrap the center with the 3" length; glue for a bow tie.

Watermelon Bag

one 5"x9"x3" glossy green bag with handles
one 5"x9"x3" glossy red bag with handles
one 1"x36" strip of glossy white paper
acrylic paints: black, white, mint green
one 1"x4" compressed sponge
#3 round paintbrush
decorative scissors (deckle by Family Treasures)
glue (see page 8)

1 Cut each bag in half horizontally, 4" above the bottom (set the red bottom and green top aside to make another bag in the reverse colors). Moisten the sponge to expand it, then squeeze out most of the water. Use the edge of the sponge, dipped into green paint, to paint vertical lines 1" apart around the green bottom. Let dry.

2 Paint black watermelon seeds evenly spaced over the red bag top. (*Hint:* Load the brush with paint, press it onto the surface, then lift it off while dragging upward to make a nicely tapered seed.) Let dry, then use the tip of the brush to stroke a white curved highlight on the lower left side of each seed.

3 Use decorative scissors to trim both long edges of the white paper strip. Glue it around the top of the green bag so half extends above the bag. Slip the red bag top inside the top of the strip and glue in place.

Diagonal Dots Bag

one 7"x9"x4" glossy white bag with handles
one 7"x9"x4" glossy black bag with handles
acrylic paints: black, white
pencil with new eraser
18" of ⅝" wide red grosgrain ribbon
glue (see page 8)

Like the watermelon bag above, this one is a combination of two bags. Cut the black bag in half diagonally (save the top half to make another bag in the reverse colors). Slip the white bag inside the black bag section and glue to secure. To paint the white dots, dip the pencil eraser into a puddle of white paint and touch it to the surface of the black section; space dots randomly over the black areas. Repeat with black paint on the white areas. Tie the ribbon into a shoestring bow with 2½" loops and 4" tails; glue to the bag center.

Animal Bags

by Bonnie Dunkel

Bunnies

for each bunny:
one 8"x10½"x4½" white bag with handles
one 1³/₈" wide wood half ball
one 8½"x11" piece of white construction paper
tracing paper, pencil, transfer paper
pink acrylic paint, ½" flat paintbrush
makeup sponge
black broad-tip felt pen
glue (see page 8)
for the girl bunny:
one 3"x24" strip of pink checked fabric
for the boy bunny:
one 3"x24" strip of purple print fabric
one 6"x4" piece of white velour fabric
polyester fiberfill, needle, white thread, 6" of sisal twine
pink powdered blush, cotton swab

1 **For each bunny:** Trace the ear pattern on page 45. Cut two from white paper; turn one over. Dip the sponge into pink paint and dab along the center of each ear; let dry. Paint the half ball pink for a nose; let dry. Transfer the face pattern onto the center front of the bag (for the boy bunny, don't transfer the muzzle line). Use the pen to draw the eyebrows, eyes and the girl bunny's mouth and muzzle line. Glue the ears and nose as shown.

2 **Girl bunny:** Use the sponge to paint the cheeks as for the inner ears. Tie the fabric strip into a shoestring bow with 3" loops and 2½" tails; glue as shown.

Dog

one 8"x10½"x4½" brown bag with handles
one 1³/₈" wide wood half ball
one 8½"x11" piece of black construction paper
one 3"x24" strip of tan fabric with black dots
tracing paper, pencil, transfer paper
acrylic paints: black, pink
½" wide flat paintbrush, makeup sponge
black broad-tip felt pen
glue (see page 8)

Paint the half ball black for a nose. Trace the ear pattern and eye ring from page 45. Cut one eye ring and two ears from black paper; turn one ear over. Transfer the bear face pattern from page 43 to the bag center, but omit the eyelashes and eye highlights; space the eyes 1" apart. Use the pen to draw the mouth and eyes. Use the sponge to paint the cheeks as for the bunnies, then use the pen tip to dot freckles on each. Glue the nose, ears and eye ring as shown. Tie the fabric strip into a shoestring bow with 3" loops and 2½" tails; glue below his muzzle.

Boy bunny: Cut the oval muzzle piece from velour. Sew a running stitch ¼" inside the edge, gather it into an oval pouch and stuff firmly. Wrap the thread ends 2–3 times around the center and knot at the back. Glue below the nose for a muzzle. Blush each side and use the pen to dot freckles. Unravel the twine and separate 6–8 plies. Thread them onto the needle and sew from one side of the muzzle to the other. Remove the needle and center the twine ends to make his whiskers. Tie the fabric strip into a shoestring bow with 3" loops and 2½" tails; glue below his muzzle.

velour muzzle pattern for boy bunny ➡

bunny face

Bear

one 8"x10½"x4½" brown bag with handles
one 1⅜" wide wood half ball
brown kraft paper: one 4½" circle, one 3½"x6" piece
one 3"x24" strip of tan/black checked fabric
tracing paper, pencil, transfer paper
acrylic paints: black, pink
½" wide flat paintbrush, makeup sponge
black broad-tip felt pen, white paint pen
glue (see page 8)

bear or panda ear

Paint the half ball black for a nose. Trace the pattern and cut two ears from brown paper. Glue the ears and brown circle to the bag as shown, then transfer the face pattern so half the dashed nose placement line extends above the brown circle. Use the pen to draw the mouth, eyes, eyebrows and eyelashes. Use the paint pen to dot the eye highlights. Use the sponge to paint the cheeks as for the bunnies, then use the pen tip to dot freckles on each cheek. Glue the nose as shown. Tie the fabric strip into a shoestring bow with 3" loops and 2½" tails; glue below his muzzle.

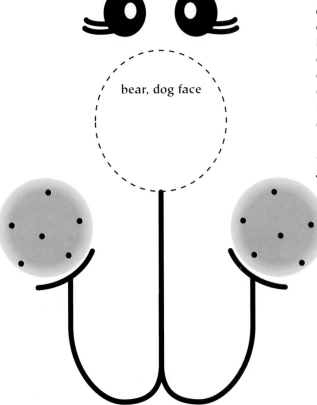

bear, dog face

Panda

one 8"x10½"x4½" white bag with handles
one 1" wide wood plug
two ½" wide black animal eyes
one 4½" circle of white paper
one 6" square of heavy black paper
one 3"x24" strip of burgundy fabric with black dots
tracing paper, pencil, transfer paper
acrylic paints: black, pink
½" wide flat paintbrush, makeup sponge
black broad-tip felt pen
glue (see page 8)

Paint the plug black for a nose. From black paper, cut two ears using the ear pattern above and two eye patches from the pattern on page 45. Glue the white circle, ears and eye patches to the bag as shown. Use the pen to draw the muzzle line ⅔ of the way down the center of the white circle. Use the sponge to paint the cheeks. Glue the nose and eyes as shown. Tie the fabric strip into a shoestring bow with 3" loops and 2½" tails; glue below his muzzle.

The kitty face pattern with whiskers, eyes, eyebrows, and ears appears on the right side of the page.

kitty face

kitty outer ear

kitty inner ear

Kitty

one 8"x10½"x4½" white bag with handles
one 1" wide wood plug
one 3½"x6" piece of white construction paper
one 2"x6 square of light pink paper
one 3"x24" strip of pink/white checked fabric
tracing paper, pencil, transfer paper
pink acrylic paint, ½" flat paintbrush, makeup sponge
black broad-tip felt pen
glue (see page 8)

Paint the plug pink for a nose. Trace the outer ear and inner ear patterns. Cut two outer ears from white paper and two inner ears from pink paper; glue as shown. Transfer the face pattern to the bag center. Use the pen to draw over the lines and fill in the eyes. Tie the fabric strip in a shoestring bow with 3" loops and 2½" tails; glue below her muzzle line.

Frog

one 8"x10½"x4½" green bag with handles
one 8½"x11" piece of green construction paper
one 3"x24" strip of green print fabric
tracing paper, pencil, transfer paper
two 1" wide wiggle eyes
pink acrylic paint, makeup sponge
black broad-tip felt pen
glue (see page 8)

Trace the pattern from page 45 onto tracing paper, cut out, unfold and transfer onto the green paper (don't transfer the dashed placement lines). Use the pen to draw over the outlines, hips, smile and eyebrows. Glue the eyes under the eyebrows. Dip the sponge into pink paint and dab on the cheeks; let dry. Use the pen tip to dot the freckles. Tie the fabric strip into a shoestring bow with 3" loops and 2½" tails; glue to his neck.

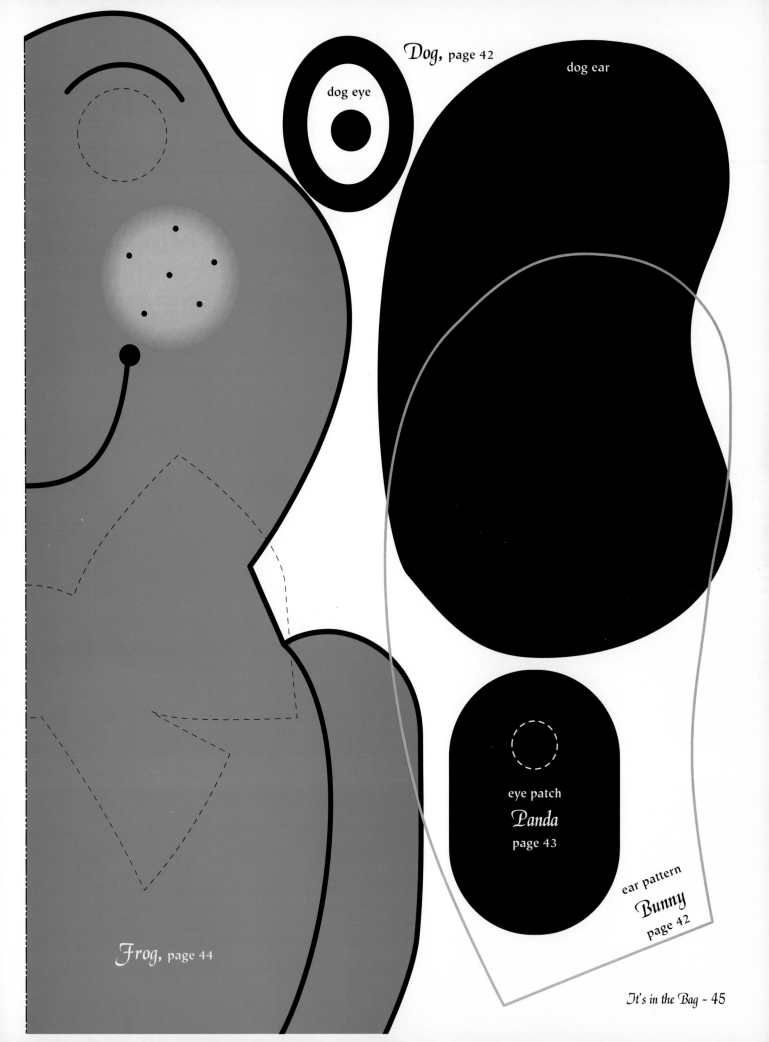

Dog, page 42

dog eye

dog ear

eye patch
Panda
page 43

ear pattern
Bunny
page 42

Frog, page 44

Halloween Bags
by Bonnie Dunkel

Transfer the face pattern to the bag. Use the pen to draw the mouth and eyes. Dip the sponge into pink paint and dab the cheeks. Paint the plug pink for a nose; let dry and glue in place. Tie the fabric strip into a shoestring bow with 3" loops and 2½" tails; glue to the top left corner of the bag.

Ghost

one 8"x10½"x4½" white bag with handles
one 3"x24" strip of orange Halloween-print fabric
one 1" wide wood plug
pink acrylic paint, ½" wide flat paintbrush
makeup sponge
black broad-tip felt pen
tracing paper, pencil, transfer paper
glue (see page 8)

Jack~O'~Lantern

one 8"x10½"x4½" orange bag with handles
one 5"x21/2" piece of black construction paper
one 3"x24" strip of orange/black checked fabric
one 1¾"x1¾"x¼" wood teardrop
acrylic paints: black, pink
½" wide flat paintbrush, makeup sponge
black broad-tip felt pen
tracing paper, pencil, transfer paper
glue (see page 8)

Transfer the eye pattern to the center of the bag, 2½" below the top edge. Draw over the lines with the pen. Dip the sponge in pink paint and dab the cheeks. Paint the teardrop black for a nose; let dry. Cut the mouth from black paper. Glue the mouth and nose as shown. Tie the fabric strip into a shoestring bow with 3" loops and 2½" tails; glue to the top left corner of the bag.

trace on fold

Monstro

one 8"x10½"x4½" green bag with handles
one 8½"x6" piece of black construction paper
one 3"x24" strip of orange/black checked fabric
one 1⅜" wide wood half ball
pink acrylic paint, ½" wide flat paintbrush
makeup sponge
black broad-tip felt pen
tracing paper, pencil, transfer paper
glue (see page 8)

hairline pattern

1 Transfer the hairline pattern to the center bottom of the black paper; cut out and discard. Trim the lower edges in a zig-zag. Glue the hair to the bag as shown. Transfer the face pattern to the bag center front, the small scar 1" right of the eyes and the large scar 1" left of the mouth. Draw over the lines with the pen.

2 Dip the sponge in pink paint and dab on the cheeks. Paint the half ball pink for a nose; let dry and glue in place. Tie the fabric strip into a shoestring bow with 3" loops and 2½" tails; glue to the bottom center of the bag.

small scar

large scar

cat ear

Black Cat

one 8"x10½"x4½" black bag with handles
one 3"x6" piece of heavy black paper
two ¾" long oval wiggle eyes
three 9" lengths of brown wired paper twist
one 3"x24" strip of orange Halloween-print fabric
one 1⅜" wide wood half ball
pink acrylic paint, ½" wide flat paintbrush
makeup sponge
white paint pen, tracing paper, pencil, white transfer paper
glue (see page 8)

Transfer the mouth pattern to the bag center front and draw over the lines with the pen. Dip the sponge in pink paint and dab on the cheeks. Paint the half ball pink for a nose; let dry. Glue the centers of the paper twist lengths at the top of the muzzle line, then glue the nose over them. Glue the eyes above the nose. Cut two ears from black paper and glue one at each top corner of the bag. Tie the fabric strip into a shoestring bow with 3" loops and 2½" tails; glue to the bottom center of the bag.

trace on fold

Scarecrow

one 7"x10"x4" tan bag with handles
one 8½"x6" piece of yellow construction paper
fourty-eight 2"–2½" lengths of raffia
one 3"x24" strip of orange/black checked fabric
one 1¾"x1¾"x¼" wood teardrop
orange acrylic paint, ½" wide flat paintbrush
broad-tip felt pens: black, red
tracing paper, pencil, transfer paper
glue (see page 8)

trace on fold

Transfer the face pattern to the bag center. Draw over the lines with the black pen. Fill in the eyes with black and the hearts with red. Paint the teardrop orange, let dry and glue in place for a nose. Glue the raffia along the top edge for hair. Trace the hat pattern from page 142. Cut the crown and brim from yellow paper; outline with dashes as shown. Glue the crown to the bag top so it extends 2¾" above the bag. Glue the brim centered over the lower edge of the crown. Tie the fabric strip into a shoestring bow with 3" loops and 2½" tails; glue to the bottom center of the bag.

tombstones →

© & ™ Accu/Cut® Systems

© & ™ Ellison®
Craft & Design

Haunted Graveyard

by Stephanie Taylor

one 8"x10½"x4½" black bag with handles
solid-color papers: black, white, yellow, brown, tan, gray
eighteen 12" lengths of raffia
ghost, spiderweb stickers (Stickopotamus®)
witch, tree die cuts (Ellison® Craft & Design)
haunted house die cut (Accu/Cut® Systems)
cloud template (All Night Media®)
silver ink stamp pad, makeup sponge
black fine-tip pen, tracing paper, pencil
glue (see page 8)

moon

trace on fold

Lay the cloud template on the bag just below the top edge. Lightly sponge silver ink over the edge of the template. Move the template down 1"–1½" and repeat; continue until a misty cloud pattern covers the top ⅔ of the bag. Trace the patterns (the tree pattern is on page 141). Cut a witch and a house from black; cut another house from white. Cut a tree from brown and one from tan. Cut the moon from yellow. Cut five tombstones from gray. Glue as shown, then embellish with stickers. Use the pen to draw details on the stones and the spider on the tree front. Hold the raffia together and knot around the right side of the handle.

Christmas Bags

by Bonnie Dunkel

Reindeer

one 7½"x10½"x4" brown bag with handles
one 4"x5" piece of tan felt
one 3"x24" strip of red/white/green print fabric
one 2" wide red pom pom
pink acrylic paint
makeup sponge
black broad-tip felt pen
white paint pen
tracing paper, pencil, transfer paper
glue (see page 8)

Transfer the face pattern to the bag center. Draw over the lines with the black pen. Fill in the eyes with black and dot the highlights with the white pen. Dip the sponge in pink paint and dab on the cheeks. Glue the pom pom for a nose. Cut two ears from tan felt. Fold a pleat in the bottom of each as shown on the pattern; glue to secure. Glue one ear to each bag corner. Tie the fabric strip into a shoestring bow with 3" loops and 2½" tails; glue to the bottom center of the bag.

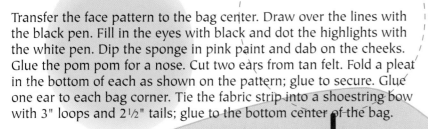

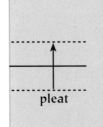

pleat

reindeer ear

Penguin

one 8"x10½"x4½" black bag with handles
one 6½"x9" piece of white paper
one 3"x24" strip of burgundy/black checked fabric
one 2" tall wood half egg
acrylic paints: pink, orange
½" wide flat paintbrush, makeup sponge
black broad-tip felt pen
tracing paper, pencil, transfer paper
glue (see page 8)

Fold a piece of tracing paper in fourths and trace the outline of the body pattern, placing the dashed lines on the folded edges. Cut out; unfold. Place on the white paper, allowing the lower curved edges to extend 2" beyond the paper; cut out. Transfer the eye pattern to the center top of the face and fill in with the pen. Glue to the bag as shown. Paint the egg orange; let dry. Invert and glue for his nose. Dip the sponge into pink paint and dab on his cheeks. Tie the fabric strip into a shoestring bow with 3" loops and 2½" tails; glue to the bottom center of the bag.

Snowman

one 8"x10½"x4½" white bag with handles
one 10"x7" piece of black construction paper
one 3"x24" strip of green fabric printed with snowflakes
one 2" tall wood half egg
acrylic paints: pink, orange
½" wide flat paintbrush, makeup sponge
black broad-tip felt pen, white paint pen
tracing paper, pencil, transfer paper
glue (see page 8)

Transfer the face pattern to the bag center. Draw over the lines with the black pen; fill in the eyes and mouth. Dip the sponge in pink paint and dab on the cheeks. Paint the teardrop orange for a nose; let dry and glue at an angle as shown. Trace the hat pattern from page 142. Cut a crown and a brim from black paper; outline with white dashes. Glue the crown to the bag top so it extends 3" above the bag. Glue the brim centered over the lower edge of the crown. Tie the fabric strip into a shoestring bow with 3" loops and 2½" tails; glue to the center bottom of the bag.

Santa eyes

Santa

one 8"x10½"x4½" tan bag with handles
two 9"x12" pieces of burgundy felt
one 8¼"x2" strip of white fake fur fabric
one 2" wide white pom pom
one 1⅜" wide wood half ball
6 yards of white acrylic yarn
pink acrylic paint
½" wide flat paintbrush
makeup sponge
black broad-tip felt pen
white paint pen
tracing paper, pencil
transfer paper
glue (see page 8)

hat

9"

¼" seam

8"

1   Transfer the eyes pattern to the bag center, 2½" below the top edge. Draw over the lines with the black pen; use the paint pen to dot white highlights. Dip the sponge in pink paint and dab on the cheeks. Paint the half ball pink; let dry and glue for a nose.

2   Follow the hat diagram to cut two 8"x9" triangles from the felt. Glue the long sides together. Let dry; turn right side out. Glue to the bag top, overlapping 1". Glue the fur for a brim. Glue the hat tip to the right as shown, then glue the pom pom to the tip. Cut the yarn into 16" lengths. Use one length to tie around the center of the others. Glue under his nose; unravel the ends for a fluffy look.

Elf

one 8"x10½"x4½" brown/tan striped bag with handles
one 7" square of tan construction one paper
two 9"x12" pieces of green felt
3"x24" strip of red fabric printed with Christmas candy
one ⅝" wide gold jingle bell
one 1⅜" wide wood half ball
6 yards of burgundy acrylic yarn
pink acrylic paint, ½" wide flat paintbrush
makeup sponge
black broad-tip felt pen
tracing paper, pencil, transfer paper
glue (see page 8)

1 Transfer the face pattern to the bag center, 2¾" below the top edge. Draw over the lines with the black pen. Dip the sponge in pink paint and dab on the cheeks. Paint the half ball pink; let dry and glue for a nose. Cut two ears from tan paper; turn one over. Use the pen to draw a curving line down the center of each, then glue one to each side of the bag as shown. Tie the fabric strip into a shoestring bow with 3" loops and 2½" tails; glue to the bottom center of the bag.

2 Follow the hat instructions in step 2 of the Santa, page 50, to make the hat. Glue the hat back to the bag front, 1" below the

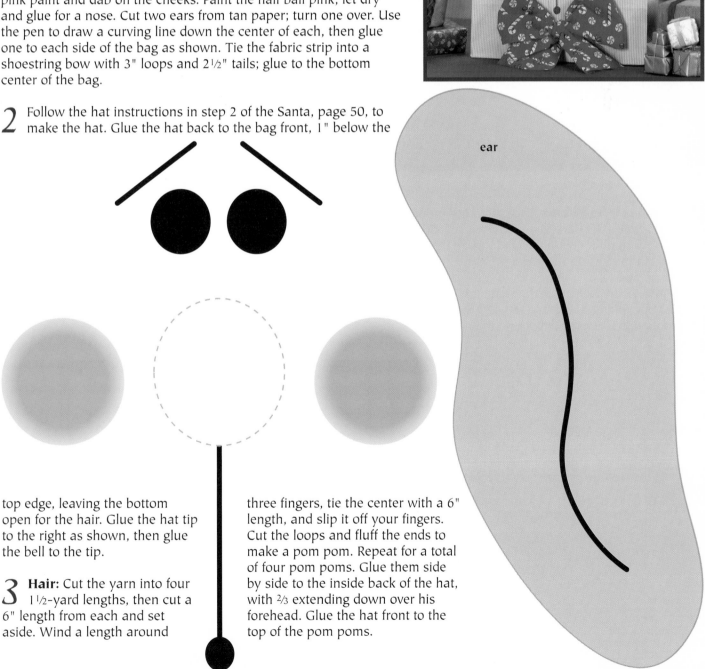

top edge, leaving the bottom open for the hair. Glue the hat tip to the right as shown, then glue the bell to the tip.

3 **Hair:** Cut the yarn into four 1½-yard lengths, then cut a 6" length from each and set aside. Wind a length around

three fingers, tie the center with a 6" length, and slip it off your fingers. Cut the loops and fluff the ends to make a pom pom. Repeat for a total of four pom poms. Glue them side by side to the inside back of the hat, with ⅔ extending down over his forehead. Glue the hat front to the top of the pom poms.

Terrific Tags

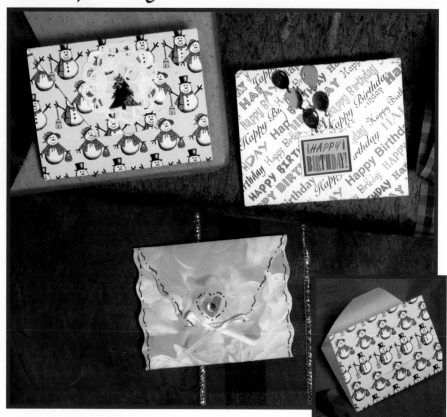

Triple-Fold Tags

by Marilyn Gossett

basic tag:
tracing paper, pencil, ruler, craft knife
one 3"x6¼" piece of cardstock
glue (see page 8)

snowman tag:
1 snowpeople card (Cards with Pizazz)
one 1½" round white paper doily
one ⅝" tall green metallic confetti tree

birthday tag:
1 happy birthday card (Cards with Pizazz)
decorative scissors (wave by Family
    Treasures)
one ¾"x1" Happy Birthday! sticker
5 metallic confetti balloons, assorted colors

rose tag:
1 pink roses card (Cards with Pizazz)
decorative scissors (wave by Family
    Treasures)
black fine-tip pen
6" of 1/16" wide ivory satin ribbon
scrap of brown paper
½" wide heart punch
one 5mm clear acrylic rhinestone

1 **To make a basic tag:** Trace the pattern onto tracing paper and cut out. Place it on the back side of the cardstock and trace lightly around it. Use the knife and ruler to cut just inside the lines. Measure and mark the fold lines; mark a 1¼" long slot in the card center ⅝" below the second fold. Cut the slot. Hold the ruler firmly against one fold line and fold the tag; repeat on the other fold line. Tuck the point into the slot.

2 **Snowman tag:** Decorate the flap with a lacy doily and a shiny tree. **Birthday tag:** Trim the flap with decorative scissors. Glue confetti balloons to the flap and attach a message sticker below the slot. **Rose tag:** Trim all the edges with decorative scissors, then draw a ~ • ~ border. Glue a bow below the slot and a heart punched from brown paper to the flap. Outline the heart and glue the rhinestone to the center.

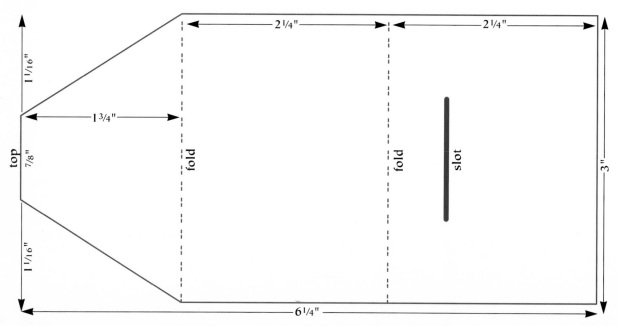

Layered Tags

by Sandy Bunka

A wonderful way to use up paper scraps, these clever and elegant gift tags are also a great craft for kids to do on their own!

papers: quilt-patterned print (MPR Paper-bilities™), brown kraft paper, scraps of papers or lightweight cardstock in assorted solids and patterns
decorative scissors (heartbeat, Victorian by Fiskars®)
black fine-tip pen, metallic gold paint pen
dimensional paints: gold glitter, orange glitter, metallic gold
1/8" hole punch (McGill, Inc.)
metallic gold thread, glue (see page 8)

1 Cut a square from the quilt paper for the top layer—trim it with decorative scissors if desired, then glue it to another piece at least 1/4" bigger all around. Use decorative scissors to trim the second layer, then glue to a third layer and trim it too. (For a different look, turn the decorative scissors upside down.) Make as many layers as you like—we used brown paper for the bottom layer on these tags.

2 Outline one or more layers with the metallic gold pen. Use dimensional paints to add outlines and dots around the hearts and stars.

3 Punch a hole in the top left corner of the tag. Insert 8" of gold thread through the hole and knot the ends. Turn the tag over and use a black pen to write your choice of message (Happy Birthday, Merry Christmas, etc.). Write "To:" and "From:" below the message.

Folded Tags

by Sandy Bunka

papers: quilt-patterned print (MPR Paper-bilities™), brown (kraft) paper, scraps of papers or lightweight cardstock in assorted solids and patterns
decorative scissors (ripple, heartbeat, Victorian by Fiskars®)
fine-tip pens: black, other colors as desired
dimensional paints: gold glitter, red glitter, blue glitter, metallic gold
1/8" hole punch (McGill, Inc.)
metallic gold thread
glue (see page 8)

1 Follow step 1 above to make a layered paper tag, but cut the brown paper layer slightly taller than the layered front and twice as wide. Fold in half, then open and use a black pen to write your choice of message (Happy Birthday, Merry Christmas, etc.) on the inside back. Write "To:" and "From:" below the message.

2 Outline one or more layers with the metallic gold pen. Use dimensional paints to add outlines and dots around the hearts and stars.Punch a hole in the top left corner of the tag. Insert 8" of gold thread through the hole and knot the ends.

Friends forever
right from the
start, caring
and sharing
from the
heart.

MERRY CHRISTMAS

Present-Perfect Boxes

This chapter shows how to make a box from paper or cardstock. You'll learn to make a square box and a rectangular box. You'll also learn how to make a puffy box (in this chapter, that is not an oxymoron!), a box with a very special lid (you'll have to make the project to see just how special the lid really is!) and a quaint little group of origami nesting boxes.

After you learn the basic technique of making a box from paper, you'll be able to adjust the size to fit your needs or use the paper that best expresses the purpose of the box. With the direction provided in the following pages, you'll be able to make a box small enough to hold a charm, or sweet enough to give for Valentine's Day.

All you need to get started is a sheet of paper or a piece of cardstock and a little dab of glue. We've given you plenty of terrific ideas to decorate each box. A bit of raffia, a scrap of handmade paper, a Punch-Out™ and a pair of decorative edged scissors go a long way in this section.

So don't wait for a gift-giving occasion. These boxes are so versatile you can use them to hold anything—from jewelry at home to paper clips at work!

Nesting Boxes

by Helen Deinema

Although they're made from paper, the folded construction of these little boxes makes them surprisingly strong. Make them in any size—the smallest shown is 1¾"x⅞"x1¾", while the largest is 4"x2"x4".

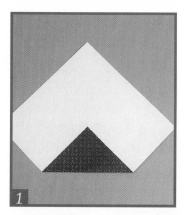

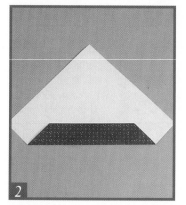

for each box:
1 square of paper for the lid
1 square of paper (matching or contrasting) for the bottom
ruler, pencil, scissors
optional: glue (see page 8)

1 **Lid:** On the back of the paper, draw two diagonal lines connecting the opposite corners, for guides. Fold one corner in to touch the center of the square.

2 Fold that corner in again to the center line.

3 Unfold; repeat steps 1 and 2 with the remaining three corners.

4 On each side of one corner, cut along the fold line across the first two cross folds. Repeat on the opposite corner.

5 Refold the uncut corners along the original fold lines, turning the box side up and tucking the cut tabs in.

6 Refold the remaining corners along the original fold lines, flattening them into the box bottom. *Optional:* Secure the inside corner points with a small amount of glue.

7 **Bottom:** Assemble exactly as for the lid, but trim the paper ⅜" smaller both ways.

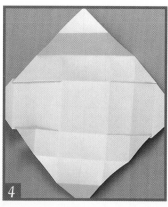

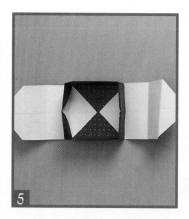

1³/₄" Green Plaid Box

5¹/₈" square of green/white plaid paper (Paper Pizazz™ Dots, Checks, Plaids & Stripes)
4³/₄" square of solid green paper
9" of ¹/₄" wide green satin ribbon

Follow the instructions on page 56 to make the box. Use the ribbon to tie a shoestring bow with 1" loops and 1" tails; glue to the box as shown.

2" Striped Box

5¹/₂" square of red/green/white striped paper (Paper Pizazz™ Papers for Cards & Envelopes)
5¹/₈" square of green paper

Follow the instructions on page 56 to make the box.

2³/₈" Red & White Plaid Box

6⁵/₈" square of red/white plaid paper (Paper Pizazz™ Ho Ho Ho!!!)
6¹/₄" square of solid red paper

Follow the instructions on page 56 to make the box.

3" Candy Box

8¹/₂" square of green paper printed with Christmas candy (Paper Pizazz™ Christmas)
8¹/₈" square of solid green paper

Follow the instructions on page 56 to make the box.

4" Red & Green Plaid Box

11¹/₂" square of red/green plaid paper (Paper Pizazz™ Christmas)
11¹/₈" square of green paper with white dots (Paper Pizazz™ Christmas)

Follow the instructions on page 56 to make the box.

Boxes from Cards

by Marilyn Gossett

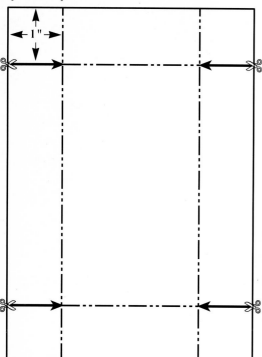

Our boxes use purchased cards, but could equally well have been made from flat cardstock covered with patterned paper (see page 14). The trimmings are limited only by your imagination!

for each box:
one 4½"x6¼" folded card (or two 4½"x6¼" pieces of cardstock)
ruler, stylus or embossing tool
double-stick tape

Cut the card along the fold; use the front for the box lid. Use the ruler and stylus to score 1" in on all edges of the card. Cut to the score line in four places as shown on the diagram. Fold on each score line, tucking the tabs inside. Secure with double-stick tape. **Bottom:** Make as for the lid, but score 1³/₃₂" from each edge so the bottom will fit inside the lid.

Ice Cream & Candles

one 4½"x6¼" birthday candles card (Cards with Pizazz)
one 2"x4½" piece of purple paper with bright dots (Paper Pizazz™ Child's Play)
one 4" tall ice cream cone (Punch-Outs™ for Kids)
decorative scissors (wave by Family Treasures)
two ³/₈" wide self-adhesive foam mounting dots
glue (see page 8)

Follow the instructions above to make the box. Glue the ice cream cone to the dotted paper, then use the decorative scissors to trim ¼" away. Use the foam dots to attach the cone to the box lid as shown.

Tie Dye & Raffia

one 4½"x6¼" tie dye card (Cards with Pizazz)
four 18" long strands of raffia
three ¾" wide metallic gold confetti suns
glue (see page 8)

Follow the instructions above to make the box. Wrap the raffia both ways around the box; tie in a shoestring bow with 1½" loops and 5" tails. Glue a sun to the bow center and one to each tail as shown.

"You're Great"

one 4½"x6¼" brown corrugated card (Cards with Pizazz)
one 3¾" wide "You're Great" plaque (Punch-Outs™ for Cards), pig and trotters (Photo Friends Punch-Outs™)
six 9" lengths of metallic gold thread

Follow the instructions above to make the box. Glue the plaque to the center top, then glue the pig head ½" above it, extending off the top of the box. Glue a trotter on each side as if the pig were holding the plaque. Hold the thread lengths together and tie into a shoestring bow with ¾" loops and 1½" tails. Glue the bow under the pig's chin.

Antique Lace Box

one 4½"x6¼" antique lace card (Cards with Pizazz)
papers: one 2" square of purple moiré (Paper Pizazz™
  Pretty Papers), one 1⅞" square of Irish chain quilt
  (Paper Pizazz™ Country)
decorative scissors (pinking by Fiskars®)
one ⅜" wide lavender ribbon rose with ribbon leaves
24" of ⅛" wide ivory satin ribbon
black fine-tip pen, glue (see page 8)

Follow the instructions on page 58 to make the box.
Wrap the ribbon both ways around the box, tying in
a shoestring bow with 1" loops and 2" tails. Glue
the quilt paper to the moiré and use decorative scissors to trim the edges; draw dashes as shown. Slip
the corner of the square under the bow; glue to
secure. Glue the rose to the bow center.

Trims & Doilies

one 4½"x6¼" trims & lace card (Cards with Pizazz)
one 3" round white paper doily
one 4mm (³⁄₁₆") clear acrylic rhinestone
three ¼" wide pink silk baby's breath blossoms
three 1" long green silk leaves
four 12" long strands of raffia, 9" of ⅛" wide ivory satin ribbon
glue (see page 8)

Follow the instructions on page 58 to make the box. Cut the
doily in half and pleat the center of each half. Glue one to the
box, then slip the other under it and glue. Use the raffia to
make a shoestring bow with 1" loops and 2½" tails; glue at the
top of the doilies. Glue the rhinestone to the bow center and
the leaves in a triangle with the blossoms in the center. Use the
ribbon to make a shoestring bow with ¾" loops and 2½" tails;
glue below the blossoms.

Hydrangeas Box

one 4½"x6¼" purple hydrangeas card (Cards with
  Pizazz)
one 3" round paper doily
four 9" long strands of raffia
two ¾" wide purple silk flowers
one 1" long sprig of purple silk lavender
one 4mm (³⁄₁₆") clear acrylic rhinestone
glue (see page 8)

Follow the instructions on page 58 to make the box.
Cut the doily in half; discard half. Pleat the center of
the other half and glue to the box. Use the raffia to
make a shoestring bow with 1" loops and 2" tails.
Glue the bow, flowers and rhinestone to the doily
top as shown.

Green Marble Box

one 4½"x6¼" green marble card (Cards with
  Pizazz)
mulberry papers: one 2½" torn square of burgundy, scraps of mauve and green
one 1"x4" strip of lavender tissue paper
two 4mm (³⁄₁₆") clear acrylic rhinestones
one 1" long sprig of white silk baby's breath, one
  ¾" wide purple silk flower, two 1½" long
  sprigs of purple silk lavender
glue (see page 8)

Follow the instructions on page 58 to make the
box. Glue the square at an angle to the top of
the box. Cut and layer the paper scraps to the
top. Cut the 1"x4" strip into ⅛" wide fringe,
pinch the end and glue to the center of the
papers, spreading the fringe to form a rosette.
Glue the flowers to the rosette center.

Shaker-Top Boxes

by Marilyn Gossett

Windowed tops can hold a variety of decorative materials—confetti, potpourri or flower petals, to name just a few. We've made them on card-stock boxes like those on pages 58–59, but they're easy to add to any box.

for each box:

one 4¹/₂"x6¹/₄" folded card (or two 4¹/₂"x6¹/₄" pieces of cardstock)
one 3¹/₂"x5" piece of paper to cover the lid
one 2³/₄"x4¹/₂" piece of foam board
one 2³/₄"x4¹/₂" piece of acetate
pencil, ruler, stylus or embossing tool, craft knife, cutting mat
double-stick tape, glue (see page 8)

1 Follow the instructions on page 58 to make the basic box from the card or cardstock. Trim the foam board to fit the box top.

2 Use the craft knife to cut the window out of the foam board, then lay it on the back side of the paper. Trace the window onto the center of the lid paper, then cut ¹/₈" inside the traced line.

3 Glue the acetate to the top of the foam board, then turn it over and position the window over the paper window. Wrap as for a gift, gluing the paper edges to the back of the foam board.

4 Fill the window with your choice of materials; glue the box top to the back of the foam board.

Rose Box & Variations

one 4¹/₂"x6¹/₄" pink roses card (Cards with Pizazz)
decorative scissors (wave by Family Treasures)

Love Letters box:
one 3¹/₂"x5" piece of letters paper (Paper Pizazz™ Black & White Photos)
2 Tbsp. of gold metallic angels confetti
3³/₄" tall heart template

Kisses box:
one 3¹/₂"x5" piece of kisses paper (Paper Pizazz™ Teen Years)
2 Tbsp. of multi-colored metallic loves & kisses confetti
3¹/₂" tall heart template

Gold & silver box:
one 3¹/₂"x5" piece of azaleas paper (Paper Pizazz™ Floral Papers)
one ⁵/₈" wide brass heart charm
9" of ¹/₄" wide gold metallic grosgrain ribbon
15" of gold/silver metallic twisted braid
1 Tbsp. of gold metallic angels confetti
1 Tbsp. of silver metallic stars confetti
1 tsp. of iridescent clear glitter
3³/₈" tall oval template

Use the template to make the window; cut out the paper window with the decorative scissors. Cover the lid with the patterned paper and fill with the confetti. **Gold & silver box:** Add the glitter to the confetti. Beginning at the center top, glue the braid around the outer edge of the box top. Glue the charm at the center top of the window. Use the ribbon to make a shoestring bow with 1" loops and 1¹/₂" tails; glue at the top of the charm to cover the braid ends.

Blue Corrugated Box

one 4½"x6¼" rainbow tie dye card (Cards with Pizazz)
one 3½"x5" piece of blue corrugated paper (Paper Pizazz™ Country)
one 3" wide "Thinking of You" plaque (Punch-Outs™ for Cards)
2 Tbsp. of gold metallic stars confetti
2" tall balloon template
one ³⁄₈" wide pale yellow ribbon rose with green ribbon leaves
two 9" lengths of ¹⁄₈" wide pink satin ribbon

Use the balloon template to make the window; cover the lid with the corrugated paper. Glue the "Thinking of You" plaque diagonally across the top left corner. Loop and glue one ribbon length from the bottom of the balloon across the lower left corner, then across the lower side of the box. Use the remaining ribbon to tie a shoestring bow with ½" loops and 1" tails; glue over the top of the looped ribbon. Glue the rose above the bow center.

Christmas House Box

one 4½"x6¼" snowflakes card (Cards with Pizazz)
one 4" wide gingerbread house (Paper Pizazz™ Quick & Easy)
one 1¼" wide red metallic confetti "MERRY CHRISTMAS"
one 1³⁄₄" tall green metallic confetti tree
1 tsp. of green metallic tree confetti
1 tsp. of gold metallic star confetti

Trim the four panes out of the paper house window. Use the house as a pattern to cut the foam board and the acetate—cut the foam board panes exactly the size of the house panes, but cut away the center moldings between the panes. Glue the acetate to the front of the foam board and the paper house to the front of the acetate. Glue the 1³⁄₄" tree to the left side of the house. Fill the window with confetti, then glue the box lid to the back of the house so the snow extends slightly beyond the bottom of the box.

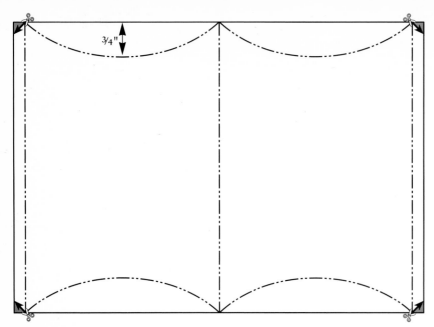

¾"

Gift Pockets

by Marilyn Gossett

These elegant pockets with gracefully curved ends are great for odd-shaped items.

for each box:
one 4½"x6¼" folded card
ruler, stylus or embossing tool
double-stick tape or glue (see page 8)

1 Open the card and lay it patterned side down. Use the ruler and stylus to score ¼" from each 6¼" card edge. Score two curved lines from fold to fold on each long edge of the card. (**Tip:** To make a smooth curve, find a plate or bowl which has about the right diameter to score along—the depth of the curve does not need to be exactly ¾".)

2 Clip off the shaded corners diagonally. Crease the 6¼" edges to the inside along the scored lines, then gently fold the card along the curved score lines (it may be easier to fold it first to the outside, then to the inside). Close the card and glue or tape the straight edges together. Bow the pocket outward, folding the curved edges in until they overlap slightly. Tie or tape to secure.

Hearts pocket:
one 4½"x6¼" puffy hearts card (Cards with Pizazz)
one 2¾" wide "Friends forever" heart, three 1⅛"–1⅜" wide puffy hearts (Punch-Outs™ for Cards)
1 yard of ⅛" wide ivory satin ribbon

Christmas pocket:
one 4½"x6¼" Christmas candy card (Cards with Pizazz)
one 2¾"x3¾" piece of red/white plaid paper (Paper Pizazz™ Ho Ho Ho!!!)
one 1" square of red paper
cutouts: one 3" tall gingerbread boy, one 3" long candy cane, one ⅞" wide heart (Paper Pizazz™ Ho Ho Ho!!!)
decorative scissors (pinking by Fiskars®), ½" wide heart punch (Family Treasures)
four 24" long strands of raffia

Floral pocket:
one 4½"x6¼" purple hydrangeas card (Cards with Pizazz)
one ½" wide brass heart charm
4" of ⅜" wide pink satin picot ribbon
1 yard of 6" wide white tulle
one 2" long sprig of purple silk forget-me-nots with six ½" wide blossoms
decorative scissors (wave by Family Treasures)

Hearts pocket: Glue the hearts as shown; tie with the ribbon, making a shoestring bow with 1¼" loops and 3" tails. **Christmas pocket:** Use decorative scissors to trim the paper; glue to the pocket center. Glue the boy to the paper holding the cane. Tie with raffia, making a shoestring bow with 2" loops and 4"–5" tails. Glue the green heart to the bow; punch a red heart and glue to the green heart. **Floral pocket:** Before scoring, use decorative scissors to trim the top and bottom edges of the card, making it a 4½" square. Tie with tulle in a shoestring bow with 2" loops and 2½" tails. Fold the ribbon into a loop and glue below the bow; glue the flowers and charm as shown.

Square Fold-Ups

by Marilyn Gossett

for each box:
one 8"x11" piece of lightweight poster board
tracing paper, pencil, 1/4" hole punch
ruler, stylus or embossing tool, spray adhesive

purple quilt box:
one 8½"x11" piece of lavender quilt paper (Paper Pizazz™)
one 12" piece of 1/4" wide mauve satin ribbon
one 3/8" wide lavender ribbon rose with green ribbon leaves
one 1" wide wood birdhouse button
acrylic paints: violet, black, white, royal blue
fine-tip black permanent pen, gloss acrylic sealer
paintbrushes: 1/2" flat, #0 liner
decorative scissors (pinking by Fiskars®)

Christmas candy box:
one 8½"x11" piece of Christmas candy paper (Paper Pizazz™)
12" of 1/4" wide gold metallic grosgrain ribbon
three 1¼" wide circular motifs from a white paper doily
3 chocolate kisses in Christmas-colored foil
decorative scissors (pinking by Fiskars®)

party box:
one 8½"x11" piece of birthday party paper (Paper Pizazz™)
3" candle, 3" balloon (Birthday Punch-Outs™)
four 9" lengths of yellow curling ribbon, ribbon shredder
12" of 1/8" wide purple satin ribbon

1 Use spray adhesive to adhere the back side of the paper to the poster-board. Using the measurements given in the diagram, make a pattern. Lay it on the back side of the posterboard and trace around it, then cut out. Cut diagonally into the inside corners as shown. Use a ruler and stylus to score the box along the fold lines. Fold on the scored lines and glue the seams together. **Quilt box:** Use the pen to outline the lid with —•—•. Paint the button violet. Use the liner to paint white lines on the roof and black stripes on the house front. Dot a blue door; highlight with a small white dot. Seal; let dry. Glue to the lid center. Paint a green pole below the house. Glue the rose to the pole bottom. Tag: Use decorative scissors to cut a 2¼"x4½" piece from a scrap of covered posterboard. Fold in half and punch a hole in the upper corner. Handle: Punch a hole in each side of the box, ½" below the top edge. Tie a triple knot in one ribbon end. Thread the ribbon through one hole, inside out. Push it through the hole of the tag, then through the opposite hole of the box; knot on the inside.

2 **Christmas box:** Follow step 1 to make the box and a tag. Punch a hole in the center flap and two in the box, one directly under the first hole and one below the flap. Thread the ribbon through the box holes, inserting the top tail through the flap hole and the tag. Tie in a shoestring bow with 1" loops and 3" tails. Glue the doily motifs and kisses to the lid as shown.

3 **Party box:** Follow step 2 to punch and tie the lid. Glue the candle to a posterboard scrap; cut out. Cut a slit in the box lid, then glue the candle into the slit. Hold the ribbon lengths together, knot the center, curl and shred. Glue to the box in front of the candle. Glue the balloon to the box front.

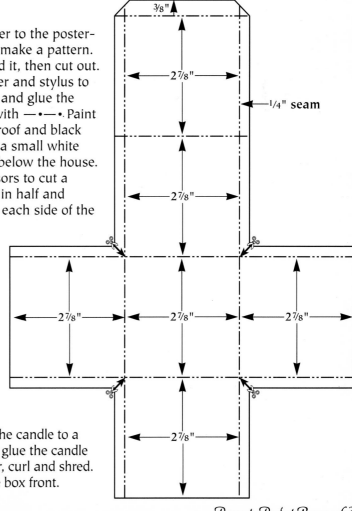

Home Decor with Style & More

Paper crafts can provide wonderful colors and textures within your home. These designs will show how to make the most of your papercrafting. Whether for your front door, your fireplace mantel or your refrigerator, these designs bring the home-spun feeling of crafted paper into your home.

This chapter teaches a great technique for using Punch-Outs™ or stickers. With a magnet strip adhered to the back, they become adorable refrigerator magnets—great gifts that even children can make themselves. You'll also learn how easy it is to decorate a photo mat with punches to suit any season or occasion. Coordinate your photos with their frames without spending a fortune!

The art of paper etching is featured in this section. The look is elegant, as you will see. And of course, the timeless technique of decoupage is offered here. You'll be surprised at the different looks you can achieve with just the right paper.

For decorating your home and more, this chapter is full of ideas for crafting with paper!

*Decoupage Plates

by Deborah Spofford

for each plate:
one 8" wide clear glass plate
gloss decoupage glue (Delta)
gloss acrylic sealer (Delta)
1/2" wide flat paintbrush
black fine-tip permanent pen
tracing paper, pencil, newspapers

Thoroughly wash and dry the plate. Protect your work surface with newspapers. Coat the plate back with decoupage glue; let dry. Add any drawn embellishments. Coat the back of the plate with decoupage glue where you will add paper embellishments, then apply while still wet; let dry. Coat the back of the plate with glue again and apply the large background paper piece. Let dry, then trim the paper to fit the plate. Seal.

* For decorative use only

Heart Plate

mulberry paper: one 9" square of purple, one 3 1/2"x3" piece of white, one 3 1/4"x2 3/4" piece of blue

After coating the plate with glue, draw a wavy line around the outer rim. Use the patterns to cut a small heart out of blue paper and a large heart out of white, then cut the remaining blue paper into many pieces. Place the blue heart in the center of the plate, the white heart over it and the pieces around the wavy line. Finish with the large square of purple.

Star Plate

mulberry paper: one 9" square of blue, one 4" square of pink
1/4" hole punch

After coating the plate with glue, draw a jagged line around the outer rim. Use the patterns to cut three stars out of pink paper and punch many circles from the remaining pink paper. Place the stars in the center of the plate and the punches around the jagged line. Finish with the large square of blue.

Polka Dot Plate

mulberry paper: one 9" square of pink, one 6" square of white, one 3" square of purple
decorative scissors (pinking by Fiskars®)

Use the decorative scissors to cut the white paper into many circles and ovals. Cut the purple into many small triangles or rectangles. Apply to the plate and finish with the large square of pink.

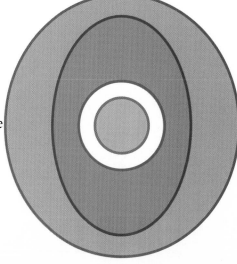

Striped Plate

mulberry paper: one 9" square of white, one 3 3/4"x9" square of pink, one 5" square of purple
decorative scissors (pinking by Fiskars®)

Use the decorative scissors to cut the pink paper into five strips. Cut the purple into many 1/2" circles. Apply to the plate as shown and finish with the large square of white.

Decoupage Frames

by Deborah Spofford

for each frame:
gloss decoupage glue (Delta)
gloss acrylic sealer (Delta)
½" wide flat paintbrush
craft knife, newspapers

for the blue frame:
one 2¾"x3½" wood picture frame
one 4¾"x5½" piece of blue mulberry paper

for the purple frame:
one 3½"x4½" wood picture frame
one 5½"x6½" piece of blue mulberry paper

1 Protect your work surface with newspapers. Remove the back and glass from the frame. Cover the frame with glue, then lay the mulberry paper over the frame. Press the paper to the frame and fold in the corners as if you were wrapping a package, using additional glue to hold them in place.

2 Use the knife to cut a large X in the center of the paper, then wrap the paper around the inside edges of the frame. Trim the excess paper in the back. Cover the paper with glue; let dry. Seal, let dry, then reassemble the frame.

Decoupage Candle Holder

by Deborah Spofford

one 2½"x2½"x3½" wide clear glass votive candle holder
mulberry paper: one 12"x4" piece of purple,
   one 6"x2" piece of blue
gloss decoupage glue (Delta)
gloss acrylic sealer (Delta)
decorative scissors (pinking by Fiskars®)
½" wide flat paintbrush
tracing paper, pencil, newspapers

Protect your work surface with newspapers. Trace the pattern. Use the decorative scissors to cut four hearts from blue paper. Cover the candle holder with glue, then lay one heart centered on each side. Press the purple paper onto the side of the holder and fold the lower corners under as if you were wrapping a package, using additional glue to hold them in place. Wrap the excess paper over the top of the candle holder to the inside. Cover the paper with glue; let dry; seal.

*Reverse Decoupage Rose Set

by LeNae Gerig

one 7 1/2" wide octagonal glass bowl
one 2 3/4"x2 3/4" glass candle holder
10" of 1/8" wide gold elastic ribbon
one 3/4" tall brass rose charm
two 8 1/2"x11" sheets of pink roses paper (Paper
    Pizazz™ Holidays & Seasons)
gold acrylic paint, 1" wide flat paintbrush
Aleene's reverse collage glue
newspapers

1   Protect your work surface with newspapers.
    Thoroughly wash and dry both glass pieces.
Bowl: Cut the paper into free-form shapes
smaller than 3"x3". Cover each piece with collage glue and place patterned side down on the
outside of the bowl, overlapping as needed to
completely cover the glass.

2   **Candle holder:** Cut the leftover paper into
    shapes smaller than 2"x2". Coat each piece
with glue and place on the inside of the candle
holder, patterned side against the glass, to completely cover it.

3   Apply another coat of glue over the paper on
    each piece; let dry for 24 hours. Paint over
the glue with gold paint. Tie the ribbon around
the candle holder; glue the charm to the knot.

Dainty Doily Pot

by LeNae Gerig

one 6 1/2" wide terra cotta pot
one 9 3/4"x14" white paper doily placemat
four 4" wide cream paper heart doilies
21" of 1/2" wide white satin picot ribbon
28" of 1/16" wide ivory satin ribbon
acrylic paints: cream, white
satin acrylic sealer, 1" wide foam paintbrush
decoupage glue, newspapers

1   Protect your work surface with newspapers. Seal the
    inside and outside of the pot. Paint the inside and rim
cream and the rest of the pot white; let dry, then seal
again.

2   Cut a 1 1/4" wide strip from the border of the placemat.
    Glue around the outer rim, finished edge down. Glue
the heart doilies shoulder to shoulder around the pot. Cut
the ivory ribbon into four 7" lengths and tie each into a
shoestring bow with 1 1/4" loops and 1 1/2" tails.

3   Use decoupage glue to attach each bow to a heart as
    shown. Glue the white ribbon around the upper edge
of the rim. (**Note:** If the pot is to be used for a growing
plant, use a plastic liner; inner moisture may cause the
decoupage glue to loosen.)

Triangle Letters Box

by LeNae Gerig

one 6¾"x6"x4½" triangular wood box
one 1" wide round gold knob with ¼" screw
one 8½"x11" sheet of letters paper (Paper Pizazz™ for
    Black & White Photos)
antique gold acrylic paint, oak wood stain
clean cloth, paper plate, paper towel, newspapers
decoupage glue, matte acrylic sealer
½" wide flat paintbrush, drill with ¼" bit

1 Protect your work surface with newspapers. Paint the lower half of the box gold; let dry.

2 Cut the paper into many irregular pieces smaller than 2"x3". Cover small areas of the lid with glue, then place paper pieces in the glue, overlapping them; repeat to completely cover the lid. Wet the brush and blot nearly dry on a paper towel. Dip into the gold paint, then blot on the towel. Lightly brush over the lid edges; let dry. Use the brush to stain the box, then use the cloth to remove excess stain. Let dry and seal. Drill a hole in the center top of the box and screw in the knob.

Angel Saucer

by Katie Hacker

one 4¼" wide terra cotta saucer
one 3" circle of angel giftwrap
one 1" wide brass angel charm
1½ yards of ⅛" wide ivory satin ribbon
7" of 22-gauge wire
gold acrylic paint, matte acrylic sealer
decoupage glue
½" wide flat paintbrush
3" wide circle template
newspapers

1 Protect your work surface with newspapers. Seal the inside and outside of the saucer. Paint the inside and rim gold; let dry, then seal. Use the template to cut a circle from the angel paper. Cover the inner bottom of the saucer with glue, then place the angel paper over it. Coat it again with glue.

2 **Hanger:** Cut two 7" lengths of ribbon, cross the ends together and glue to the top back of the saucer. Measure 4" from one end of the remaining ribbon, then loop it back and forth to make eight 2" loops (four on each side). Wrap the center with wire, twist tightly at the back and trim the second tail to 4". Glue to the lower saucer, then glue the charm to the center.

Children's Easy Decoupage Dresser Set

by LeNae Gerig & Katie Hacker

for each piece:
tissue paper: red, orange, yellow, green, blue, purple
decoupage glue
1" wide flat paintbrush

dresser:
5-drawer wood dresser
primer paint
black matte latex paint
medium-grit sandpaper
2" wide flat paintbrush
clean cloth

lampshade:
one 10" high Cool Shades Lampshade Kit (includes precut
   lampshade paper and metal frame)
stapler

frame:
one 11"x12$^{1}/_{2}$" unfinished wood frame with a 4$^{1}/_{2}$"x6$^{1}/_{2}$"
   opening
primer paint
black matte latex paint
medium-grit sandpaper
2" wide flat paintbrush, clean cloth
ruler, pencil

Dresser

Remove the knobs from the drawers and the drawers from the chest. Lightly sand all pieces; wipe off dust. Paint the chest, drawer fronts and knobs with primer; let dry and sand lightly; wipe off dust. Paint black; let dry. Cut the tissue into 1"–2" triangles. Cover each drawer front with decoupage glue, a small area at a time, and place tissue triangles in the glue. (To keep a straight edge around the drawer fronts, glue triangles along the straight edges

first, then fill the remaining area with overlapping pieces.) Apply a final coat of decoupage glue as a sealer; let dry. Replace the knobs and drawers.

Lampshade

Follow the kit instructions to assemble the shade. Cut the tissue into 1"–2" triangles. Cover the shade with decoupage glue, a small area at a time, and place tissue pieces in the glue, aligning the edges of the triangles with the straight edges of the shade. Fill in the remaining area with overlapping pieces. Apply a final coat of decoupage glue as a sealer; let dry.

Frame

Lightly sand the frame and paint with primer; let dry and sand again; wipe off dust. Paint the frame black; let dry. Measure and mark a line 1" from the frame opening. Cover from the line to the outer edge with decoupage glue, a small area at a time. Apply triangles, aligning their straight edges with the pencil line and the frame edge. Fill in the remaining area; let dry. Apply a final coat of decoupage glue as a sealer; let dry.

Mosaic Terra Cotta Pot

by Becky Goughnour

one 6½" wide terra cotta pot
papers: one 3"x7" piece of navy tri-dots, one 4"x6" piece of
    burgundy with white dots (Paper Pizazz™ Dots, Checks,
    Plaids & Stripes), one 3"x10" piece of metallic gold (Paper
    Pizazz™ Metallic Papers), one 2"x4" piece of handmade-look
    green (Paper Pizazz™ Handmade Papers)
4" wide heart template, pencil
white acrylic paint, matte acrylic sealer, 1" wide flat paintbrush
newspapers, decoupage glue

1 Protect your work surface with newspapers. Seal the
inside and outside of the pot; let dry, then paint
white. Tear the blue paper into fourteen ¾"–1"x1½"
strips. Tear fourteen ½"–¾"x1½" pieces of gold paper.
Use the decoupage glue to cover the pot rim, a small area
at a time, and place strips evenly spaced around it, alternating colors. Use the template to lightly draw a large
heart on the pot front; repeat on the back. Tear eighty ½"
squares of burgundy paper. Cover a heart with glue and
press 40 burgundy pieces diagonally inside the heart,
leaving spaces between them; repeat for the other heart.

2 Tear eight ¼"x2¾" gold strips and eight ½"x½" green
squares. Cover the areas between hearts with glue
and place four green squares diagonally on each side as
shown to form diamonds. Glue four gold strips to frame
them. Apply a final coat of decoupage glue to the entire
pot; let dry. (**Note:** If the pot is to be used for a growing
plant, use a plastic liner; inner moisture may cause the
decoupage glue to loosen.)

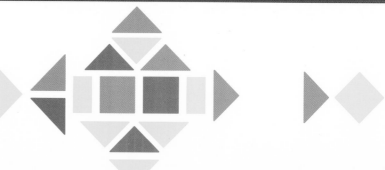

Mosaic Fish Tray

by LeNae Gerig

one 11½"x5½"x1½" wood tray
8½"x11" papers: blue, aqua, light aqua, green, yel-
    low, apricot, orange
⅝" square punch (Marvy® Uchida)
green paint, acrylic wood sealer
1" wide paintbrush
decoupage glue, newspapers

1 Protect your work surface with newspapers.
Seal the tray; let dry. Paint green, let dry and
seal again. Punch many squares from each paper.
Cover the center of one tray side with glue, then
place a row of alternating green, blue aqua and
light aqua squares diagonally along it. Repeat
around the outside and inside of the tray.

2 Cover the bottom of the tray with decoupage
glue, a small area at a time. Follow the patterns to make three large and three small fish in
the bottom of the tray—vary the colors as
shown, and cut squares into triangles or strips
as needed. Use the remaining green, blue and
aqua pieces to cover the rest of the tray bottom.
Be sure to leave spaces between the paper
pieces for a mosaic look. Apply a final coat of
decoupage glue as a sealer; let dry.

Corrugated Wall Hanging

by LeNae Gerig

one 10½" square of navy blue cardstock
corrugated paper: one 10" square of dark green, four
*   3½"x4" pieces of burgundy, one 5"x3" piece of dark green*
four 2" long wood heart cutouts
navy blue acrylic paint
½" wide flat paintbrush
2 yards of jute twine
tracing paper, pencil
glue (see page 8)

1 Glue the 10" square paper to the cardstock. Glue the burgundy pieces evenly spaced over the 10" square as shown. Trace the heart pattern, cut out, then trace it four times on the back of the green corrugated; cut out. Glue one to the center of each burgundy piece.

2 Paint the hearts blue; let dry. Glue one to the center of each green heart. Cut four 9" lengths of jute and tie each into a shoestring bow with ¾" loops and 2" tails. Knot each tail and trim to 1½" long. Glue one to the top of each navy heart. Cut the remaining jute into three 12" lengths. Glue the ends of one to the top corners of the hanging to make a hanger. Use the remaining lengths to make shoestring bows with 1" loops and 2" tails. Glue the bows over the hanger ends.

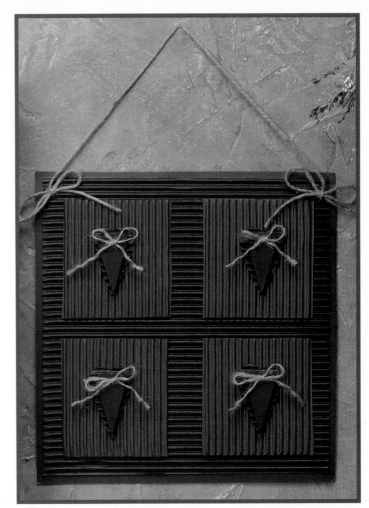

Corrugated Box

by LeNae Gerig

one 4" wide round papier-mâché box
corrugated paper: one 4" square of dark green,
*   one ½"x15" strip of dark green, one ¾"x15"*
*   strip of burgundy, one 1¼"x15" strip of bur-*
*   gundy, one 1½"x2½" piece of burgundy*
one 2" long wood heart cutout
9" of jute twine
navy blue acrylic paint, ½" wide flat paintbrush
glue (see page 8)

1 Paint the heart and box bottom blue; let dry. Trace the lid onto the back of the green paper, cut out and glue in place. Glue the ¾"x15" burgundy strip around the lid edge. Glue the 1¼" burgundy strip to the center of the box with the ½"x15" green strip in the center of the burgundy.

2 Trace the heart pattern above, cut out, then trace onto the back of the small burgundy corrugated piece; cut out and glue to the lid center. Glue the wood heart to the center of the burgundy heart. Use the jute to make a shoestring bow with 1" loops and 2" tails. Knot the tails, trim to 1½" and glue to the heart as shown.

Quilted Welcome Wall Hanging

by Sandy Bunka

one 4⅝"x12½" piece of cream mat board
one 8½"x11" piece of quilt-block patterned paper in muted blues, greens, burgundy and tan with hearts and stars (MPR Paperbilities™)
wood pieces: one 7" wide banner, five ¾" long hearts, one ¼" long heart
acrylic paints: navy blue, burgundy
matte spray sealer, 1" wide flat paintbrush
½"–⅝" wide buttons: 1 blue, 1 tan, 1 burgundy
three 2½" lengths of white pearl cotton thread
twelve 1" long sprigs of white dried German statice
two 1" tufts of Spanish moss
seven ½" long blue paper rosebuds
ten ⅛" wide burgundy berries
24" of 18-gauge wire, ruler, drill with ⅛" bit
black permanent pens: fine-tip, broad-tip
glue (see page 8)

1 Paint the banner and two ¾" hearts blue; paint the remaining hearts burgundy; let dry. Glue a burgundy heart to each side of the banner, then drill a hole above and below it. Wrap the wire around the paintbrush handle. Insert each end through the top hole, then back through the bottom hole so 1½" extends. Wrap the end around the paintbrush again to coil it. Glue the banner to the top of the mat board.

2 Cut three 2¼"x2¾" and three 1⅛"x2¼" patches from the quilt paper. Glue onto the mat board as shown. Glue the remaining wood hearts between the papers. Insert a length of thread through each button and knot in front. Glue a button to the center of each 2¼" patch. Use the fine pen to draw squiggly dashed lines around the 2¼" patches and - -\-/- -around the 1⅛" patches. Draw a solid border around each pair of patches as shown, then a dashed line around each border.

3 Outline each wood heart with a different border. Draw a bow on each banner heart and one near each remaining large heart. Draw a squiggly dashed line around the banner, then use the broad pen to write "Welcome" in the center. Use the fine pen to draw dashes around each letter. Seal. Glue moss below the banner and the statice, rosebuds and berries into the moss.

Pastel Wall Quilt

by Katie Hacker

solid papers: one 12" square of white, one 5" square of
    white, one 8½" square of yellow, one 8¼" square of light
    green, twenty-one 1" squares of assorted pastel colors,
    twelve ¼" squares of assorted pastel colors
assorted pastel patterned papers: four 1"x11" strips, twelve
    2" squares, two 1½"x6" strips (Paper Pizazz™ Light Great
    Backgrounds, Country)
one 16" long twig
¼" hole punch, compass or circle cutter
glue (see page 8)

1 Glue the yellow square to the center of the white
   square, then glue the 11" strips around the edges of
the yellow square, overlapping the ends as shown.

2 Glue the 1" squares to the 5" white square in a
   checkerboard pattern. Use the punch to make 12
assorted ¼" dots and glue to cover the corners of the
squares. Use the compass to draw a 4¼" circle over the
squares and cut it out. Glue to the center
of the 8¼" green square.

3 Use the pattern above to cut twelve shapes from assorted colors. Glue
   them around the 4¼" circle as shown. Trim the square ⅛" away, following the shapes of the paper pieces, then glue it to the center of the yellow square. Glue one end of each 1½"x6" patterned strip to the top front of
the white square, 3" from the corner, and the other end to the back. Insert
the twig into the loops.

Fall Leaves Hanging

by Katie Hacker

© & ™ Accu/Cut® Systems, Inc.

three 3½" squares of cardstock
handmade papers: one 3" torn square of green, one 3" torn square of bur-
    gundy, one 3" torn square of blue, one 2"x21" strip of mauve
three 4" squares of cedar handmade-look paper (Paper Pizazz™ Handmade
    Papers)
3" wide leaf die cuts: 1 mauve, 1 green, 1 brown (Accu/Cut®)
twig pieces: two 2" lengths of ⅛" thick, 6½" of ¼" thick
18" of jute twine
black fine-tip pen, glue (see page 8)

1 Cover the cardstock squares with cedar paper, wrapping the edges
   to the back as if wrapping a package; glue to secure. Glue a handmade square diagonally to each cedar square, then glue a leaf to each
handmade square, varying the angles.

2 Cut one end of the mauve strip in an inverted "V." Fold 1" of the
   other end back and glue, forming a loop. Slip the 6½" twig through
the loop. Glue the top square 1" below the fold, then glue the remaining
squares 2" apart below the first.

3 Knot a 4" jute length around the center of each 2" twig; glue
   between the squares as shown. Hanger: Tie a 1" loop in each end
of the remaining jute. Slip one loop over each end of the top twig.

Seasonal Photo Mats

by LeNae Gerig

Super-simple seasonal decorating—just change the mat on your favorite photo!

Spring

one 8"x10" ivory mat with a 4½"x6½" opening
2"x3" piece of pink/white checked paper (Paper Patch®)
3"x8½" strips of solid paper: green, light green, pink, light pink, pink, light blue, aqua, lavender, yellow, white
punches: 1¼" long hand, ½" wide shamrock, 1/16" round, ¼" round (McGill, Inc.); 3/8" wide heart, ¼" leaf, ¼" wide flower, 3/8" wide flower, 3/8" long teardrop (Family Treasures)
black fine-tip pen, glue (see page 8)

Use the pen to draw vines and squiggles around the mat opening. Glue flowers and leaves (see below) around the vines. Punch two plaid hands and glue light green cuffs to each. Glue to the bottom right of the mat. **For each daisy:** Punch four white hearts and glue in a circle, points together. Punch a ¼" circle and glue to the center. **Buds:** Punch aqua and pink teardrops. **Flowers:** Punch blue ¼" circles and glue 1/16" white circles to them. Punch pink, white and lavender flowers and glue white or yellow 1/16" circles in the centers. **Greenery:** Punch green and light green leaves and green shamrocks. Draw a vein line in each shamrock center.

Summer

one 8"x10" white mat with a 4½"x6½" opening
3"x5" patterned paper strips: navy blue with white dots, red with white stars, navy blue/white checked, red/white checked (Paper Patch®)
1"x8½" solid paper strips: navy blue, red
punches: ¾" wide heart, ½" wide star (Family Treasures)
black fine-tip pen, glue (see page 8)

Punch 3–5 hearts from each paper and cut each into thirds. Reassemble into 17 hearts, varying the combinations as shown. Glue evenly spaced around the frame. Punch nine red and eight navy stars; glue between the hearts. Connect the hearts and stars with a swirling —•—• line. Draw a similar border around the mat edges.

Autumn

one 8"x10" ivory mat with a 4½"x6½" opening
3"x5" solid paper pieces: brown, rust, dark green, purple, golden yellow
punches: 5/8" long maple leaf, ¼" long leaf, 5/8" long oak leaf, 1¼" long oak leaf (Family Treasures); 1¼" long leaf (McGill, Inc.)
black fine-tip pen, glue (see page 8)

Use the pen to draw wavy lines and dots around the mat opening. Punch the leaves from different colors. Glue as shown, piling them more heavily at the bottom left. Glue fewer leaves farther apart as they move away from the corner, as if they were falling into the pile.

Winter

one 8"x10" white mat with a 4 1/2"x6 1/2" opening
solid papers: 3"x6" piece of green, 3"x6" piece of dark green,
   2"x3" piece of red
punches: 5/8" long maple leaf (Family Treasures), 1" wide bow,
   1/4" round (McGill, Inc.)
glue (see page 8)

Punch leaves from both green papers and glue randomly around the inside edge to resemble holly. Punch and glue clusters of 1–3 red circles for berries. Punch and glue a red bow at the center top.

Dogwood Mat

one 5"x7" mauve mat with a 3"x4 1/2" opening
solid papers: 3"x8" piece of cream, 1"x2" piece of burgundy, 2 1/2"x8 1/2" piece
   of dark green
punches: 1 1/4" long balloon (Family Treasures); 1 1/4" long leaf, 1/4" round
   (McGill, Inc.)
black fine-tip pen, glue (see page 8)

1 **For each flower:** Punch four cream balloons. Use the round punch to punch a half circle out of the top of each balloon. Use the pen to draw vein lines and outlines on each. Glue in a circle, bottoms overlapping as shown. Glue five burgundy circles in a pile in the center.

2 Punch six green leaves and use the pen to draw a vein line on each. Glue the leaves and flowers in opposite corners of the mat. Use the pen to draw tendrils and dots around the flowers and leaves.

Ladybugs Mat

one 5"x7" white mat with a 3"x4 1/2" opening
black/white plaid paper: two 1/2"x3" strips, two 1/2"x6" strips (Paper Patch®)
solid papers: 2 1/2"x5" piece of red, 2"x5" piece of black
punches: 1 1/4" round (Family Treasures), 1/2" round, 1/16" round (McGill, Inc.)
black fine-tip pen, glue (see page 8)

1 **For each ladybug:** Cut a 1 1/4" red circle in half to make wings. Punch several 1/16" holes in each half. Glue the wings over a 1 1/4" black circle, angled apart as shown. Glue a 1/2" black circle for the head. **For the half ladybugs:** Cut a 1 1/4" red circle in half and punch several 1/16" holes in each half. Cut a 1 1/4" black circle in half. Offset a black half behind each wing. Glue a 1/2" black circle tucked slightly under the forward curve of each wing.

2 Glue the plaid strips around the inner edges of the mat. Glue the ladybugs to the mat as shown. Use the pen to draw antennae and make dotted trails between the ladybugs.

Cream Velvet Box

by LeNae Gerig

one 8" round papier-mâché box
Velvet Paper™: one 8¹/₂" square, one 3¹/₂"x 25" strip (SilkPaint Corp.)
Paper-Etch Dissolving Gel® (SilkPaint Corp.)
Victorian Frames stencil (StenSource Int'l. Inc.)
52" of ¹/₂" wide cream gimp braid
26" of 1" wide cream satin ribbon
1³/₄" wide brass bow charm
ivory acrylic paint, matte acrylic sealer, ¹/₂" wide flat paintbrush
paper towels, iron, old toothbrush
masking tape, thin tacky craft glue

1 Trace the box top on the back of the paper square and cut out. Place the stencil over the circle and tape in place. Follow the manufacturer's directions to apply dissolving gel to the paper through the stencil. Remove the stencil from the circle and make dots and swirls around the outside of the paper; let dry. Tape the center of one side of the stencil to the center of the paper strip. Apply the dissolving gel, remove the stencil and add dots around the design; repeat for the length of the strip. Let dry.

2 Follow the manufacturer's directions to heat the back of the paper. Rinse under running water, using the toothbrush to gently brush away paper bits. Remove excess water with paper towels and iron dry.

3 Use the paintbrush to apply glue to the back of the paper. Glue the circle to the box lid and the strip around the side.

Glue the ribbon around the bottom edge of the lid. Glue a row of braid around the top lid edge and another row around the bottom of the box.

4 Wash the charm with soap and water; let dry. Paint it ivory, then rub off most of the paint with paper towels; let dry and seal. Glue the charm to the center of the lid.

pattern for
Velvet Lampshade
page 79

Velvet Lampshade
by LeNae Gerig

one 4½" tall lampshade kit (Cool Shades) which includes
   precut lampshade paper and metal frame
one 5¼"x18" strip of Velvet Paper™ (SilkPaint Corp.)
Paper-Etch Dissolving Gel® (SilkPaint Corp.)
watercolor paints: light pink, dark pink, light green, dark green
paintbrushes: ½" wide flat, #8 round
decorative scissors (seagull by Fiskars®)
iron, old toothbrush, stapler, thin tacky craft glue

1 Trace around the lampshade paper on the back of the
   velvet paper. Use the decorative scissors to trim the
top and bottom edges of the velvet paper. Trim the sides
with straight scissors.

2 Place the velvet paper over the rose pattern on page
   78, then over a light source such as a window, light
box, or sheet of glass over a flashlight. Follow the manufacturer's instructions to trace the rose pattern with dissolving gel three times across the paper. Embellish the
design with groups of three dots in the empty areas; let
dry. Follow step 2 on page 78 to remove the excess velvet
from the pattern.

3 Dilute light pink paint with an equal amount of water
   and use the round brush to apply it lightly to the rose;
repeat with light green paint on the leaves. The velvet
paper will absorb and spread the paint quickly. While the
paint is still wet, shade the rose and leaves with diluted
dark pink and green; let dry.

4 Use the flat brush to apply glue to the shade paper.
   Smooth it onto the back of the velvet paper; let dry.
Overlap the sides ½", stapling at the top and bottom.
Place the shade over the wire frame and mount on a lamp.

Pink Gingham Frame
by Anne-Marie Spencer

one 10"x7½"x1¼" sheet of Styrofoam®
1 yard of 4" wide pink gingham paper ribbon
1 teatime cutout (Paper Pizazz™ Child's Play)
1¾ yards of ⅜" wide pink/white gimp braid
1½" wide organza ribbon: 1¼ yards each of pink and yellow
7" of 22-gauge wire
serrated knife, ruler, pencil, glue (see page 8)

1 Mark 1¼" from each edge of the foam, then use the
   knife to cut out the center. Cut two 10" and two 7½"
paper ribbon lengths. Glue a 10" length to each long side of
the frame—glue the outside first, then trim to fit as you
wrap to the inside. Use 7½" lengths
for the top and bottom. Cut two 10"
and two 7½" lengths of braid; glue
around the outer front. Cut two 7½"
and two 5¼" braid lengths and glue
around the inner front. Glue the tea
set at the lower left.

2 **Bow:** Hold the ribbons together
   and wrap one end around your
thumb to make a center loop. Fold
back and forth to make a 2½" and a
3" loop on each side of your thumb.
Bring the end up and hold behind
your thumb. Insert the wire through
the center loop and twist the ends
tightly—be sure to catch all the
ribbon ends. Cut the long loop into
8" tails. Glue the bow to the frame,
draping the tails as shown.

Paper Rose Projects

by LeNae Gerig

for each project:
*handmade variegated tissue-like
    paper: pink, white*
*brass charms: one 1" long cherub,
    one ¾" long key*
gold acrylic paint, silver spray glitter
paper towels, paper plate
½" wide flat paintbrush
thin tacky craft glue

for the box:
*one 3¼"x1½"x5" wide papier-
    mâché book box*

for the frame:
*one 5"x7" papier-mâché frame
    with a 3½" wide heart opening*

for the ornament:
*one 4" wide round papier-mâché
    ornament with gold hanger*

1 **Box:** Paint the box, except the top of the lid, gold. Let dry. Moisten the tissue with water and gently tear into irregular 1" wide shapes, 5–6 of each color. Brush glue onto the paper and apply randomly to the box; let dry. Cut sixteen ½"x8" strips of pink tissue. Follow the directions below to make each rose. Glue the paper roses to the box top in the shape of a heart; let dry. *To finish:* Dip the paintbrush in gold paint, blot nearly dry on paper towels, then brush gently onto the box top and onto each rose. Glue the charms as shown and lightly spray glitter over the box; let dry.

2 **Frame:** Paint the entire frame gold. Follow step 1 to apply tissue pieces to the frame front, then to make 24 roses; glue around the inner edges of the frame. Follow step 1 to finish. **Ornament:** Paint the ornament gold. Follow step 1 to make fifteen roses; glue to the ornament center in the shape of a heart. Finish as before.

To Make a Rose:

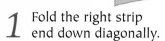

1 Fold the right strip end down diagonally.

2 Tightly roll the strip two turns to the left, then fold the right end back and down. Holding the tail firmly, roll another half turn toward the left.

3 Fold the right end back and down again. Continue to roll and fold until there is only a 1" tail remaining on the left.

4 Hold the tails together and twist. Dip into glue and press onto the project.

Rose Frame
by LeNae Gerig

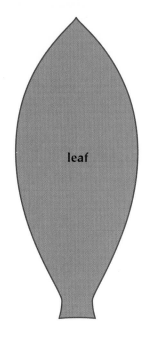

leaf

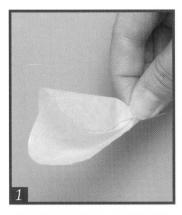

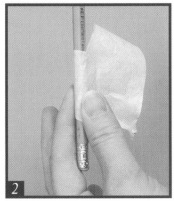

petal

13"x11" green stained wood frame with a 4½"x7"opening
handmade papers: pink, green
three 36" long strands of raffia
gold acrylic paint, old toothbrush
green floral tape, tracing paper, pencil, glue (see page 8)

1 Trace the patterns. Cut seven petals from pink paper; cut two leaves and nine ½" wide strips, 6"–12" long, from the green paper. To make the center of the rose, roll a petal into a tight cylinder around a pencil and pinch the bottom. Wrap a second petal around the first.

2 Wrap the shoulders of the remaining hearts tightly around the center of a pencil to curl them. Place the petals around the rolled center, spacing evenly and overlapping. Pinch the bottom of each petal around the center and hold it tightly. Add the leaves to the base of the rose, pinch tightly and wrap the base several times with floral tape.

3 Use the raffia to make a shoestring bow with 2½" loops and 9" tails. Knot the tails 1½" from each end. Glue the bow to the upper left corner of the frame and glue the rose to the bow center. Wrap each green strip tightly around the pencil to make tendrils; glue among the raffia loops and tails. Moisten the toothbrush with water, dip in gold paint, pull back the bristles and spatter lightly over the frame. Let dry.

Green Wood Frame

by Katie Hacker

one 10" square green wood frame with a 3" square opening
one 2"x10" piece of oatmeal handmade-look paper (Paper Pizazz™ Solid Muted Colors)
one 5½" long oatmeal oak leaf die cut (Accu/Cut® Systems)
black fine-tip permanent pen, black calligraphy pen
one 2½" long twig
one 16mm (⅝") green/gold glass bead
10" of 1mm hemp twine
one 2¾" tall fairy cutout (Artifacts, Inc.)
ruler, glue (see page 8)
matte acrylic sealer, 1" wide flat paintbrush, sandpaper, newspapers, soft cloth

© & ™
Accu/Cut®
Systems, Inc.

1 Lightly sand the frame, then wipe off the dust. Seal. Hold the ruler firmly against the oatmeal paper strip, ¼" from one edge, and tear the edge off; repeat on the other side, so the strip measures 1½" wide. Glue to the center left side of the frame. Glue the leaf diagonally to the lower right corner.

2 Glue the fairy to the strip 1" below the frame top. Knot one end of the hemp, then slide the bead onto the hemp to the knot. Wrap the hemp around the twig until the bead hangs down ½"; glue to secure. Glue the twig ½" below the sticker.

3 Use the fine-tip pen to write "Magic happens every day...Magic happens every day..." in a curved line above the frame opening. Use the calligraphy pen to write "I believe..." on the leaf.

Triptych Wall Hanging

by Katie Hacker

papers: 5½"x17" torn strip of dark green corrugated handmade (MPR Paperbilities™), three 4" torn squares of ivory handmade, three 2¾" torn squares of light green handmade
brass charms: ¾"x1¼" moon, 1"x1½" butterfly, ½"x¾" fish (Creative Beginnings)
four 36" long strands of raffia
glue (see page 8)

1 Fold the top 1½" of the corrugated strip back and glue at the bottom, forming a casing. Glue an ivory paper square 1½" below the top, then glue the remaining ivory squares ½" apart below the first. Glue a green square to the center of each ivory square. Glue a charm to the center of each green square.

2 Cut six 12" raffia lengths. Hold two together and tie in a shoestring bow with 1½" loops and 2" tails; repeat twice. Glue a bow to the top of each green square. **Hanger:** Thread the remaining raffia through the casing and tie in a shoestring bow with 3" loops and 5" tails.

sticker by The Gifted Line®

sticker by The Gifted Line®

sticker by The Gifted Line®

sticker by The Gifted Line®

sticker by The Gifted Line®

sticker by The Gifted Line®

sticker by The Gifted Line®

sticker by The Gifted Line®

sticker by The Gifted Line®

Congratulations!

Best Friends

Tea Time!

Tea Time Friends

Paper Pizazz™ Photo Friends Punch-Outs™

Paper Pizazz™ Photo Friends Punch-Outs™

Paper Pizazz™ Punch-Outs™ for Christmas Cards

Paper Pizazz™ Baby Punch-Outs™

Paper Pizazz™ Punch-Outs™ for Christmas Cards

Paper Pizazz™ Photo Friends Punch-Outs™

Magnets

by Marilyn Gossett

graphic image (such as a sticker, cutout, or Punch-Out™)
piece of self-adhesive magnetic sheet slightly larger than the image
heavy-duty sharp scissors
optional: decorative scissors, laser or inkjet printer, dimensional sealer, small embellishments such as buttons, bows or confetti

Image embellishments: (1) Glue on a message, printed or handwritten on a piece of white paper, then edged with decorative scissors. (2) Layer the image on one or two solid-color papers, trimming each layer slightly larger with either straight or decorative scissors. (3) Glue on confetti or other embellishments. (4) Cover the image with dimensional sealer; let dry. (For another effect, highlight parts of the image with the sealer).

Remove the backing from the sheet magnet and adhere the image to it. Cut around the image.

Journals & Books

These projects show you just how easy making a book can be. You'll find that the many types of books you can make, and the possible appearances of each, are practically endless! From simple to complex, these designs will show you how to make the perfect book for any use. Embellishing these books with charms, beads, patterned papers, ribbon, raffia, or Punch-Outs™ is easy when you use the ideas in this chapter.

Charming three-fold books, designed with cardstock and patterned papers, are embellished with matted photos or personal messages to be revealed whenever you need to see them most. A hand-stitched design uses corrugated paper to make the cover and brown kraft paper for the inside pages. The cover is designed with hand-made paper and old postage stamps. Journals are created by decorating the covers of spiral-bound journals with all manners of gorgeous accents. Photos can be matted and framed on the cover, or charms that add a personal touch can be glued to it.

These books can be tailored to your own purposes and used for such things as a brag book for grandma or desktop decoration for the workplace. They could make a great personal or gift diary, or maybe a daily log of exercise or golf scores. Create a memory album to be filled with photos, a recipe book or a notebook for a special class. As you craft each book with care you'll find that the outside of the book will become as meaningful as whatever the inside comes to hold.

Mini Gift Books
by Katie Hacker

Always & Forever

papers: one 11"x6" piece of lace & ribbons (Paper Pizazz™ Romantic Papers), one 5"x7" piece of white rosebuds (Paper Pizazz™ Floral Papers), one 5"x7" piece of green handmade-look (Paper Pizazz™ Handmade Papers), one 5" piece of gold metallic (Paper Pizazz™ Metallic Papers), one 8½"x11" piece of ivory
one ½" wide brass heart charm (Creative Beginnings)
ten 4" lengths of gold angel hair
13" of ⅛" wide ivory satin ribbon
computer with laser or inkjet printer and script font (or hand-letter with a calligraphy pen)
2 photos, color photocopier
circle cutter or template with 1¼", 1½", 1⅞" and 2½" circles
decorative scissors (scallop by Fiskars®)
glue (see page 8)

1   Photocopy your photos, reducing them if necessary, and cut each into a 1½" circle. Use the computer to print "True Love" and "Always & Forever" on the ivory paper, centering each in two lines. Cut each into a 1¼" square.

2   Fold the lace paper in half lengthwise, back side together, and glue. With the folded edge at the top, fold the right side in 2¾", then fold twice more. Turn so the single page is on top. Cut the photos into 1½" circles, glue to rosebuds paper and use the decorative scissors to trim ¼" larger. Glue each photo to a 1⅞" green circle. Glue to the two inside center sections as shown below.

3   Cut two 1½"x2" green strips and trim the long edges with decorative scissors. Glue to rosebuds paper, trimming them ⅛" larger on each side and even on the top and bottom. Glue to gold paper and trim 1/16" away. Glue the printed squares to the green strips, then glue to the inside left and right sections as shown below.

4   Cut a 1¼" green handmade-look circle, trim with the decorative scissors and glue to a 1½" gold paper circle. Glue to rosebuds paper and trim ½" larger with decorative scissors. Mount on a 2½" gold paper circle. Fold the angel hair in half and insert one end through the eye of the charm; knot to secure. Glue to the green circle. Place the ribbon across the center front of the book with 4" extending off the right side. Glue the circle to the book front over the ribbon. Close the book and tie the ribbon in a knot.

Dear Friend

papers: one 10"x4" piece of purple daisies (Paper Pizazz™ Floral Papers), one 1¾"x5" piece of ivory, one 1½"x4" piece of lavender
decorative scissors (cotton candy by Fiskars®)
1¼ yards of 1/16" wide purple satin ribbon
1⅜" oval template
purple fine-tip pen, glue (see page 8)

Fold the daisies paper in half lengthwise, back side together, and glue. With the folded edge at the top, fold accordion-style every 2". Cut four 1⅜" lavender ovals, glue each to ivory paper and use the decorative scissors to trim ⅛" larger. Write "I am" "so thankful" "for you," and "dear friend" on successive ovals, then glue one to each inside section as shown below. Use the ribbon to tie four shoestring bows, each with ½" loops and ½" tails and glue one to the top of each circle. Tie the remaining ribbon around the outside of the book to close it.

Happy Birthday

papers: one 8⅜"x6" piece of "Year full of delight" paper cut so the saying is at the bottom right (Paper Pizazz™ Inspirations & Celebrations), one 8½"x11" piece of oatmeal handmade-look paper (Paper Pizazz™ Solid Muted Colors), three 1"x2½" torn strips of pink handmade-look paper (Paper Pizazz™ Handmade Papers), three 2"x2½" pieces of green, three 2⅛"x1⅝" pieces of lavender
12" of ⅛" wide ivory satin ribbon
computer with laser or inkjet printer and script font (or hand-letter with a calligraphy pen)
⅛" hole punch (McGill, Inc.), ruler, glue (see page 8)

Fold the "Year of delight" paper in half lengthwise, back side together; glue to secure. With the fold at the top and the saying on the back, fold the right side in 2⅝", then fold the left side over. Use the computer and oatmeal paper to print "Wishing you all these" centered in three lines, and "good things and more" and "Happy Birthday" centered in two lines. Tearing against the edge of a ruler, tear out each printed section. Refer to the lower photo to layer the paper pieces on the inside sections. Punch a hole 1/16" from the right edge through all three layers, insert the ribbon and knot.

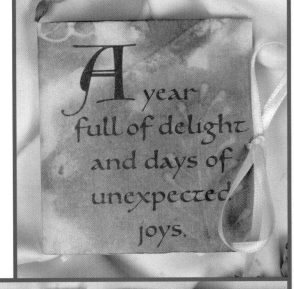

Mini Photo Albums

by Katie Hacker

Amanda & Auntie Lynda

one 6"x4" piece of white cardstock
papers: one 5¾"x3¾" and one 6½"x4½" piece of multi-colored handmade-look (Paper Pizazz™ Inspirations &
  Celebrations), one 10"x7" and one 2"x3" piece of handmade-look with dried flowers, one 5"x8½" and one 2"x3"
  piece of mauve handmade-look, one 2"x6" piece of burgundy
  handmade-look, 1⅝" square of blue handmade-look (Paper
  Pizazz™ Handmade Papers)
two 8" lengths of ¹⁄₁₆" wide purple satin ribbon
decorative scissors (ripple by Fiskars®)
4 photos, reduced to 2" on a color photocopier
purple pens: fine-tip, medium-tip
pencil, ruler, stylus or embossing tool
circle cutter or 2" circle template, 1⅝" tall oval template
glue (see page 8)

1 **Book cover:** Use the ruler and stylus to score two lines ¼" apart in the center of the cardstock for the book spine. Glue the 6½"x4½" piece of multi paper to the outside of the cardstock, folding the edges in and folding out excess at the corners. Glue 1" of one ribbon end to the inside center of each 4" edge. Glue the 5¾"x3¾" piece of multi paper to the inside, covering the ribbon ends and paper edges.

2 **Inner fold-out:** Fold the 10"x7" piece of flowers paper in half lengthwise, back side together; glue to secure. With the fold at the top, fold accordion-style into four sections. Glue to the right inside back of the book, with the left edge butting against the spine fold so the insert unfolds to the right.

3 Cut two photos into 2" circles and two into 1⅞" squares. Glue the round photos to mauve paper and the squares to burgundy paper; use the decorative scissors to trim ⅛" away. Glue the squares to mauve paper and use straight scissors to trim ¹⁄₁₆" away. Glue the matted photos to the inside book sections as shown below. Fold the photo sections closed.

3 **Inner plaque:** Cut out a heart, glue it to the blue square, then double-mat the square on burgundy and mauve, trimming the burgundy layer with decorative scissors. Glue to the front panel of the photo fold-out. **Front plaque:** Cut an oval and glue it to flowers paper; use decorative scissors to trim ⅛" away. Repeat with burgundy paper. Use the broad pen to write your choice of names, then use the fine pen to draw decorative squiggles above and below the writing. Glue to the album front. Tie the ribbons in a shoestring bow to close the album.

Generations

one 7"x4½" piece of cardstock
papers: one 7½"x5" piece of antique lace, one 6"x4" piece of antique lace, one 11"x8½" piece of burgundy moiré (Paper Pizazz™ Black & White Photos), one 7"x8½" piece of green, one 3½"x4½" piece of ivory
24 black photo corners
two 12" lengths of ¹⁄₁₆" wide burgundy satin ribbon
1⅛" wide brass bow charm (Creative Beginnings)
2¾"and 3⅛" oval templates
4 photos, reduced to 2"x3" on a color photocopier (a color copier gives better results, even with black-and-white photos)
black fine-tip pen, pencil, ruler, stylus or embossing tool

Make the book and fold-out like the one on page 88. Crop the photos, glue them to green paper and trim ¹⁄₁₆" away. Use ivory ovals on green rectangles for the front and inner plaques. Mount each piece with photo corners for a vintage look.

Sunflowers

one 5½"x3" piece of cardstock
papers: one 6"x3½" and one 5"x2½" piece of yellow daisies (Paper Pizazz™ Floral Papers), one 9½"x5" piece of blue denim (Paper Pizazz™ Country), one 5"x7" piece of yellow, one 3"x8½" piece of green
three 3" tall sunflower stickers (©Mrs. Grossman's Paper Co.)
two 14" lengths of ⅛" wide green satin ribbon
2 photos, reduced to about 2" on a color photocopier
decorative scissors (mini scallop by Fiskars®)
circle cutter or 1⅞" circle template
black fine-tip pen, pencil, ruler, stylus or embossing tool

Make the book and fold-out like the one on page 88. Crop the photos in circles, glue them to yellow paper and trim ⅛" away. Cut the sunflower heads out and stick them to green paper; trim ⅛" away; repeat with yellow. Glue two sunflowers and the photos to the fold-out as shown below. Cut a yellow circle for the inner plaque and decorate with a half sunflower with leaf. Add a leaf to the remaining sunflower and mat again on green for the front plaque.

Accordion-Fold Books
by Katie Hacker

for each book:
one 11"x4½" piece of cardstock
ruler, craft knife, glue (see page 8)

Use the ruler and knife to score the cardstock vertically every 2⅝". Fold accordion-style, then unfold and follow the project directions to cover and complete.

Sticks & Beads

papers: one 11½"x5" piece of fern handmade-look, one 10½"x4½" piece of green handmade-look, one 10½"x3½" piece of natural handmade-look (Paper Pizazz™ Handmade Papers), one 11"x1" torn strip of green corrugated handmade (MPR Paperbilities™)
two 2" long twigs
1 yard of 2mm hemp twine
green marble-look beads: two 12mm, one 7mm
green fine-tip pen
matches or lighter

1 Glue the fern paper to the outside of the cardstock, folding the edges in and folding out excess at the corners. Glue the green handmade-look paper to the inside, covering the cut paper edges. Glue the corrugat-ed strip horizontally across the center. Carefully refold accordion-style on the score lines.

2 Cut four 2½"x3½" pieces of natural paper. Carefully burn the edges until each is small enough to fit in the book. Write "I will make" "each day" "a new" and "beginning" on successive pieces; glue one to each inside section as shown below.

3 Cut an 18" twine length. Wrap several times around one twig, then place a 12mm bead on the twine. Wrap around the other twig piece, leaving 1½" between the two. Add the remaining beads and knot as shown. Glue to the book front. Cut two 12" twine lengths, tie each in a knot and slide over the left and right book edges to hold it closed.

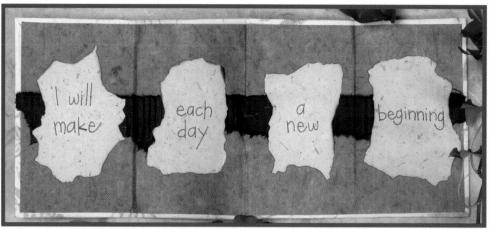

Elk Lake

*papers: one 11¹/₂"x5" piece of seashells (Paper Pizazz™ Inspirations &
Celebrations), one 10¹/₂"x4" and one 2"x2¹/₂" piece of blue handmade-look,
one 4"x11" piece of tan handmade-look, (Paper Pizazz™ Handmade Papers),
one 8"x8¹/₂" piece of purple*
4 photos, reduced to 2¹/₂"x3¹/₂" on a color photocopier
corner rounder (Marvy® Uchida), decorative scissors (deckle by Family Treasures)
two 9" long strands of raffia, black fine-tip pen, pencil
template with 2¹/₄", 2⁵/₈" and 3¹/₈" ovals

Follow the instructions on page 90 to make the book. Trim the photos into
ovals, mat and glue as shown below. For the front plaque, use the decorative
scissors to cut a 2¹/₄" oval of tan paper. Glue to a 2³/₈"x1¹/₂" round-cornered
purple piece, then glue to blue paper and trim ¹/₈" away with straight scissors.
Close the book, wrap a raffia strand around the top, knot the ends and trim
closely.
Repeat
around the
bottom.
Slip the raffia
loops off to
open the
book.

Bubbles Thank You Book

*papers: one 2"x2¹/₂" piece of bright bubbles, one 10¹/₂"x4" and one 5¹/₂"x1¹/₄"
strip of purple chalky (Paper Pizazz™ Bright Great Backgrounds)*
5¹/₂" of ³/₈" wide silver iridescent sparkle self-adhesive ribbon
12" of ¹/₁₆" wide purple satin ribbon
¹/₂" wide silver coil charm
black fine-tip pen

Follow the instructions on page 90 to make the book. Write "You make me
happy when skies are gray! Thank you!" on the inside as shown. Glue the 5¹/₂"
purple strip to the front section, ¹/₄" from the top edge, wrapping the left half
around to the back. Adhere the silver ribbon on top. Close the book, wrap the
purple ribbon around it and tie in a shoestring bow with the charm in the center. Slip the ribbon off to open the book.

Books from Cards

by Katie Hacker

Gran's Brag Book

two 4½"x6¼" purple swirl folded cards (Cards with Pizazz)
papers: two 4½"x6¼" pieces and one 1"x3" strip of purple
    sponged (Paper Pizazz™ Pretty Papers), five 4½"x½"
    strips of purple with white dots (Paper Pizazz™ Papers for
    Cards & Envelopes), one 8½" square each of lavender,
    purple and white
22" of ¹⁄₁₆" wide purple satin ribbon
3 color photocopies of photos, each 3" wide
decorative scissors (ripply by McGill, Inc.)
½" wide heart punch (Family Treasures)
corner rounder (Marvy® Uchida)
purple pens: fine-tip, broad-tip
¹⁄₁₆" hole punch (McGill, Inc.)
circle cutter or 3⅛" circle template, pencil, glue (see page 8)

1 Refold the cards so the patterns are on the insides. Open one and lay it flat. Glue the left flap of another card over the right flap of the open card so you have three sections as shown. Cover the backs of the left and right flaps with the 4½"x6¼" paper pieces.

2 Cut the photos into 3⅛" circles, then cut one lavender circle the same size. Glue all the circles to solid purple paper and trim ¼" larger with the decorative scissors. Cut four 3⅝" white squares and four 3⅞" lavender squares. Round the corners of each square, then glue the white ones to the lavender ones. Glue one circle to each white square. Punch sixteen hearts from the remaining sponged paper; glue one into the corner of each white square. Glue a photo square into each inside section and the remaining square to the book front.

3 Cut five 4½"x¾" lavender paper strips; glue a dotted strip to the center of each. Glue one to the bottom of each photo panel, ⅛" above the edge, and one to bottom front and bottom back. Close the book and use the hole punch to punch two holes ¹⁄₁₆" apart ¹⁄₁₆" from the right edge. Thread 12" of ribbon through the holes and tie in a shoestring bow. Tie the remaining ribbon in a shoestring bow with ¾" loops and ¾" tails; glue to the book front above the journaling mat. Use the broad pen to write "Gran's Brag book" on the lavender circle and to make a ▬•▬ border around the circle. Use the fine pen to make a similar border around each white square and to write the baby's name.

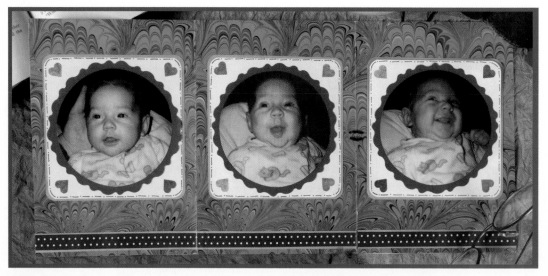

Just Wanted to Tell You

two 4½"x6¼" hearts, coils & stars folded cards (Cards with Pizazz)
papers: two 4½"x6¼" pieces of bright stripes on black (Paper Pizazz™ Papers
    for Cards & Envelopes)
3¼" wide heart die cuts: 1 blue, 1 yellow, 1 magenta, 1 lime (Accu/Cut®
    Systems)
2¼" wide star die cuts: 2 blue, 3 yellow, 2 lime, 1 magenta (Accu/Cut®
    Systems)
⅛" wide line stickers: yellow, blue, light blue, lavender, orange (Design Lines
    ©Mrs. Grossman's Paper Co.)
12" of ¼" wide white satin ribbon
black fine-tip pen, ¼" hole punch (McGill, Inc.)

heart, star © & ™
Accu/Cut® Systems

Follow step 1 on page 92 to make the book. Referring to the photos, place two line stickers parallel to the top front and three at the bottom. Open the book and place two vertically inside the left edge and three along the right edge. Write "Just wanted to tell you—" on one heart and "You are" "so special" and "to me" on the others. Glue as shown. Draw spirals and rays on the stars, then glue them among the hearts. Close the book and punch a hole 1/16" from the center front edge through all the layers. Thread the ribbon through the holes and tie in a shoestring bow.

You Remain an Original

two 4½"x6¼" rainbow tie-dye folded cards (Cards with Pizazz)
papers: two 4½"x6¼" pieces and six ¼"x4½" strips of mauve handmade-
    look (Paper Pizazz™ Handmade Papers), six ½"x4½" strips of metallic gold
    (Paper Pizazz™ Metallic Papers), one 1¼" square of oatmeal handmade-
    look (Paper Pizazz™ Solid Muted Colors), 1"x6¼" strip of dark green
    handmade corrugated (MPR Paperbilities™), one 1¾" square of light green
    handmade, one 1¼"x6¼" piece of burgundy, one 1½"x6¼" strip of purple
sun letter seal, gold sealing wax
black fine-tip pen, black broad-tip pen, metallic gold paint pen
two 20" lengths of metallic gold ribbon

Follow step 1 on page 92 to make the book. Glue gold paper strips along the top and bottom edges of the inside, then glue mauve strips along the centers. Referring to the inside photo, write "In a world full of copies, you remain an ORIGINAL" on the inside. Glue the remaining paper strips layered in the center front of the card. Glue the squares diagonally over them, then imprint a wax seal. Refer to the photo to draw gold rays and dots, then outline them with black. Tie each ribbon length in a knot and trim the ends. Slide over the top and bottom of the closed card.

Pink Roses Book

pink roses paper: two 5½" squares, two 4" squares, one
3"x4½" piece, one 2"x11" strip (Paper Pizazz™ Holidays &
Seasons)
one 2¾" square of pink moiré paper (Paper Pizazz™ Wedding)
two 4¼"x8½" pieces of pink paper
two 10" lengths of ⅛" wide pink satin ribbon
9" of ⅛" green satin ribbon
one ½" wide pink ribbon rose with green ribbon leaves
decorative scissors (deckle by Family Treasures)

Before gluing the linings, glue 1" of a pink ribbon to the
center of each closing edge. To close the finished book, tie
the ends together in a shoestring bow. Trim the moiré paper
with decorative scissors and glue to the book front. Fold the
2"x11" paper strip widthwise into ⅜" pleats, then pinch and
glue the bottom to form a fan. Glue diagonally to the book
front. Glue the rose to the fan base. Use the green ribbon to
make a shoestring bow with ¾" loops and 2" tails; glue
below the rose.

Baby Book

papers: two 5½" squares, two 4" squares and one 3"x4½"
piece of pastel stripes on pink, two 4¼"x8½" pieces and
one 3" square of pastel dots on yellow (Paper Pizazz™
Light Great Backgrounds)
1 bear, 1 pacifier (Baby Punch-Out™)
1 yard of ⅛" wide pink ribbon
decorative scissors (wave by Family Treasures)

To use printed paper for the inside pages, fold one piece
back side out and one back side in. Place the back sides
together and glue the edges. Use the ribbon to tie the pages
into the book; knot on the outside and trim the tails to 6".

Square Books
by Marilyn Gossett

for each book:
two 4½" squares of posterboard (book covers)
two 5½" squares of patterned paper (outside covering)
two 4" squares of patterned paper (inside lining)
one 3"x4½" piece of patterned paper (spine)
one or more 4¼"x8½" pieces of plain or patterned paper
  (pages)
glue (see page 8)

1 **Cover:** Lay a 5½" paper back
side up and place a posterboard
square in the center. Trim the corners of the paper diagonally, ¼"
from the corners of the posterboard.
Fold diagonally and glue to secure. Wrap and glue the
paper edges around the posterboard. Glue a 4" paper to
the inside to cover the edges. Repeat for the back cover.

2 Lay the covers side by side, ⅛"–¼" apart, insides
up. **Spine:** Fold in the long edges of the 3"x4½"
paper piece so they meet in the center; glue to secure.
Glue the binding to the inside edges of the covers. Fold
the book closed.

3 **Pages:** Fold the papers in half and place in the book
(each piece of paper will make four book pages),
one inside another, with the folds against the spine.
Glue the pages in place, or wrap a ribbon length around
the center of the pages and tie on the outside.

Use decorative scissors to trim the yellow square; glue the
square, bear and pacifier to the book front as shown.

Hydrangeas Book

*papers: two 5½", one 3", one 3½", one 1¾" and two 4"
squares of purple moiré, one 3"x4½" piece of purple moiré
(Paper Pizazz™ Pretty Papers), two 4¼"x8½" pieces of
cream parchment*
1 yard of ⅛" wide purple satin ribbon
1 yard of ⅛" wide light green satin ribbon
9" of ⅛" wide metallic gold braid
one 1" wide brass angel charm
metallic gold paint pen
pencil, 1⅝" wide heart template, 2¾" wide heart template
decorative scissors (wave by Family Treasures)

Follow the instructions on page 94 to assemble the book.
Hold the ribbon lengths together to tie in the pages; knot at
the top and trim the tails to 8" long. Trace the 1⅝" heart on
the back of the 1¾" moiré paper square and the other on
the back of the 3" hydrangea square. Use decorative scissors to cut the small heart and straight scissors to cut the
hydrangeas heart. Glue the small heart to the center of the
hydrangeas heart, then glue both to the 3½" moiré square
and use the decorative scissors to trim ¼" away. Glue the
charm to the heart center. Use the gold pen to draw a line
from the top of the charm to the top of the hydrangeas
heart, then to outline the large heart.
Use the braid to make a shoestring bow with ½"
loops and ¾" tails; glue at the top of the line.

Bridal Book

*one 8½"x11" piece of trims and charms paper, two 4"
squares and one 3"x4½" piece of white moiré (Paper
Pizazz™ Wedding)*
two 4¼"x8½" pieces of white vellum
one 4" round white paper doily
1 yard of ⅛" wide green satin ribbon

Cut two 5½" squares from the trims and charms paper,
including the decorated corners. Follow the instructions on
page 94 to assemble the book. Before gluing the linings,
glue 1" of a green ribbon length to the center of each closing edge. To close the finished book, tie the ends together in
a shoestring bow. Cut the doily into four quarters. Fold
under the straight edges of one and glue to a front corner of the book; repeat in each corner.

To the Sea

by Becky Goughnour

one 7"x10" blue spiral-bound journal (DMD Industries)
patterned papers: one 8½"x11" sheet of "I Come to the Sea" (Paper Pizazz™ Inspirations & Celebrations), one ½" square of oatmeal hand-made-look (Paper Pizazz™ Solid Muted Colors)
one 3" square of burgundy corrugated paper (MPR Paperbilities™)
solid papers: one 6¾"x10" piece of pale peach, one 6⅜"x10" piece of burgundy, one 6¼"x10" piece of dark brown, one 4" square of dark blue
brass charms: one 2" wide sun, one 1½" long fish, two ⅝" wide sand dollars (Creative Beginnings)
decorative scissors (deckle by Family Treasures)
metallic gold pen, ruler, glue (see page 8)

1 Fold one long edge of the peach paper under ¼", moisten and tear. Glue to the front of the journal with the torn edge against the binding. Glue the burgundy paper ⅛" inside the torn edge of the peach paper. Glue the brown paper ⅛" inside the burgundy, then use the ruler and pen to draw a vertical line ⅛" from one long edge. Use pattern-edged scissors to trim the left edge of the sea paper, then cut it to 6¾"x11". Glue to the journal front as shown, wrapping the edges under and folding out excess in the corners.

2 Tear the edges off the oatmeal paper, then glue it to the blue square, offset as shown. Glue diagonally to the cover just below the quote. Glue the corrugated square horizontally on top. Glue the charms as shown.

Old Letters Scrapbook

by Becky Goughnour

12" square black spiral-bound scrapbook (DMD Industries)
papers: one 12" square of brown suede-look, one 12" square of letters (Paper Pizazz™ Black & White), one 8½" torn square of burlap-look (Paper Pizazz™ Country), one 6" square of metallic gold (Paper Pizazz™ Metallic Papers), one 7" square of tan handmade-look (Paper Pizazz™ Handmade Papers), one 12" square of ivory, one 6" square of brown, one 5" torn square of black handmade, one 3½" torn square of ivory flecked handmade
11" of ¼" wide burgundy satin ribbon
12" of ⅛" wide gold bead trim
two 1¾" long brass feather plum charms (Creative Beginnings)
decorative scissors (deckle by Family Treasures)
glue (see page 8), gold sealing wax and seal, matches or lighter

1 Use the decorative scissors to trim one edge of the ivory paper; glue to the journal front with the deckle edge next to the binding. Cut the suede paper to 11¼" wide and glue it to the journal front, leaving ¼" of the deckled edge exposed. Glue the bead trim along the left edge of the suede paper.

2 Cut the gold and tan squares in half diagonally. Wrap a gold triangle around each front corner 2¾" from the corner. Fold out the excess in the corner and glue the edges inside. Repeat with the tan triangles, placing them ⅛" inside the diagonal gold edges as shown.

3 Carefully burn the edges of the letters paper until it's 11" square. Glue it to the center of the journal front, extending over the decorative corners. Glue the brown square at a slight angle to the center. Glue the burlap and handmade papers offset on top as shown.

4 Use the ribbon to make a 2" loop with 3" tails; glue to the center of the ivory paper. Follow the manufacturer's instructions to place a wax seal where the ribbons cross. Glue a charm to each front corner of the journal.

Victorian Scrapbook

by Becky Goughnour

one 9"x11" purple spiral-bound scrapbook (DMD Industries)
papers: one 12" square of flowers & charms print (Paper
    Pizazz™ Inspirations & Celebrations), two 8½"x11" pieces
    of ivory laser lace (Paper Pizazz™ Romantic Papers), one
    8½"x11" piece of metallic gold (Paper Pizazz™ Metallic
    Papers), one 3½"x5" piece of white rosebuds (Paper
    Pizazz™ Floral Papers), one 4½"x5½" piece of white
one 4½" tall Victorian dancers sticker (The Gifted Line®)
decorative scissors (seagull by Fiskars®)
13" of cream/gold twisted cord
15" of 3½" wide cream gathered lace
⅛" hole punch (McGill, Inc.)
pencil, 4⅞" tall oval template, glue (see page 8)

1. Cut the charms paper to 9½" wide and glue to the journal front; wrap the edges to the inside, folding out excess at the corners. Cut the lace section from each lace paper. Glue to gold paper and trim 1/16" away. Glue one along the binding. Cut the remaining piece in half and wrap half around each front corner, gluing inside.

2. Cut the rosebuds paper into an oval. Glue to gold paper and trim 1/16" away; glue to white and use decorative scissors to trim ⅜" away. Punch at every point of the scallop, then glue to gold paper and trim 1/16" away. Glue to the journal front and place the sticker in the center. Glue the lace around the spiral binding; tuck the ends into the open ends of the spiral. Glue the cord over the front lace edge , tucking the ends in.

Vintage Photo Journal

by Becky Goughnour

one 7"x10" white spiral-bound journal (DMD Industries)
papers: one 8½"x7" piece of ivory trims & laces (Paper Pizazz™
    Very Pretty Papers), one 9"x7" and 4"x6½" piece of metallic
    gold, (Paper Pizazz™ Metallic Papers), one 7½"x11" piece of
    burgundy
gold acrylic paint, ½" wide flat paintbrush, paper towels
12" of ½" wide ecru gimp braid
10" of ⅝" wide white taffeta ribbon with gold wired edges
4"x6" color photocopy of a black and white photo
pencil, 5⅞" tall oval template, glue (see page 8)

1. Wad the burgundy paper into a ball, then flatten it out. Dip the paintbrush into gold paint, wipe most off on paper towels, then dab gold paint onto the raised areas of the paper. Wad it and flatten it again; let dry.

2. Glue the trims paper to gold paper. Cut the photo into an oval and glue to gold paper. Trim both ⅛" larger. Glue the burgundy paper to the journal front, fold the edges inside and fold out the excess in the corners. Glue the trims paper to the center of the burgundy paper, left edge even, and glue the right edge to the inside. Glue the photo to the center.

3. Glue the braid along the binding to cover the paper edges. Tie the ribbon in a shoestring bow with 1" loops and 2" tails. Glue it to the top center of the journal front.

Baby Book

by Becky Goughnour

one 7"x10" mauve spiral-bound journal (DMD Industries)
papers: one 7½"x11" piece of cream roses (Paper Pizazz™ Pretty
  Papers), two ⅛"x11", one 1⅛"x3" piece and two ⅛"x7½"
  pieces of metallic gold, two ¼"x11" and two ¼"x7½" strips of
  metallic gold, (Paper Pizazz™ Metallic Papers), one ⅞"x2¾"
  piece of ivory, one 2¼" square of ivory, one 1"x2⅞" piece of
  light blue
3½" octagonal gold frame (Paper Pizazz™ Embellishments)
¾" tall alphabet stickers, 2" wide sleeping baby (The Gifted
  Line®)
1½ yards of ⅜" wide peach satin picot ribbon
1½ yards of ⅜" wide white satin picot ribbon
glue (see page 8)

1 Glue the roses paper to the journal front, wrapping the
   edges to the inside and folding out the excess in the corners. Glue the gold strips as shown, turning the ends inside.

2 Use the alphabet stickers to spell "BABY" on the ivory rectangle. Glue to the blue, then to the gold rectangle. Glue
2¼" below the journal top. Cut the frame center of the gold
frame out and glue the ivory square behind the opening.
Adhere the baby sticker to the ivory square, then glue to the
journal front.

3 Weave the ribbons through the spiral binding as
   shown. Tie the ends in shoestring bows with 1"
loops and 3½" tails.

Hugs & Kisses

by Katie Hacker

one 7"x10" purple spiral-bound journal (DMD Industries)
papers: one 7½"x11" piece of blue/yellow pastel plaid,
  one 4¾"x4" and one 2⅛"x10" piece of yellow with pastel dots
  (Paper Pizazz™ Light Great Backgrounds), one 4½"x3¾" and
  one 2⅝"x10" piece of purple corrugated (MPR Paperbilities™),
  one ⅝"x11" and one 4¾"x3" piece of yellow, one 5"x4¼" piece
  of purple
one 4⅜" wide "Hugs & kisses, stars for wishes" oval plaque
  (Paper Pizazz™ Sayings Punch-Outs™)
10" of ½" wide white satin picot ribbon
decorative scissors (deckle by Family Treasures)
glue (see page 8)

1 Glue the plaid paper to the journal front, wrapping the
   edges to the inside and folding out the excess in the corners. Glue the purple corrugated strip vertically to the center
front. Use the decorative scissors to trim the dotted strip,
then glue to the center of the purple. Glue the yellow strip
and the ribbon to the center of the dotted paper.

2 Glue the remaining purple corrugated to the center of
   the yellow dotted, then to the solid purple; use the
decorative scissors to trim ⅛" away. Glue diagonally to
the journal front as shown.

3 Glue the plaque to the remaining yellow paper and
   trim 1/16" away with decorative scissors. Glue to the
center of the journal.

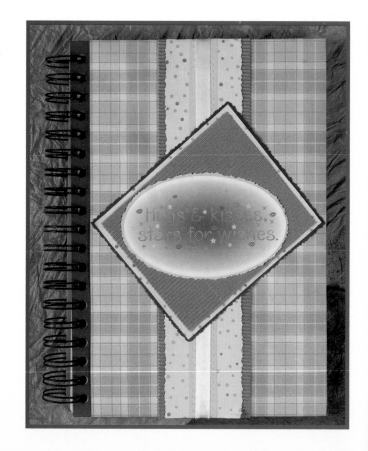

Holly Leaf Christmas Book

by Becky Goughnour

one 8"x6" silver spiral-bound journal (DMD
    Industries)
one 7"x5" photo mat with a 4½"x3" opening
6"x8" piece of silver/gold swirl paper (Paper
    Pizazz™ Metallic Papers), one 3½"x 5" piece
    of black velour paper (Hygloss)
⅛" wide metallic gold line stickers (Design
    Lines ©Mrs. Grossman's Paper Co.)
7" of ⅝" wide burgundy satin ribbon
7" of ⅜" wide metallic gold ribbon
3½"x2" brass holly charm (Creative
    Beginnings)
craft knife, cutting mat, glue (see page 8)

1 **To cover the mat:** Lay the paper back
side up and center the mat on it. Fold the
outer corners diagonally to the inside and
glue, then fold in the sides and glue. Use the
knife to cut an X in the center, cutting just to
the inside corners. Pull each section to the
back, trim excess paper and glue in place.
Turn the mat right side up and adhere a
sticker ¼" from each edge, folding the ends to the back.
Glue the black velour paper to the back so it shows
through the opening.

2 Glue the gold ribbon to the center of the burgundy
ribbon, then glue vertically to the center front of the
journal, wrapping the ends to the inside. Glue the frame to
the center front. Glue the charm to the frame center.

Fisherman's Brag Book by Becky Goughnour

one 4"x5½" brown corrugated journal (D&CC)
papers: one 5"x8⅜" piece of brown alligator-look (Paper Pizazz™ Masculine
    Papers), two 1⅞"x1¼" pieces of brown suede-look (Paper Pizazz™ Black
    & White Photos), one 2½"x3½" piece of oatmeal handmade-look (Paper
    Pizazz™ Solid Muted Colors), two 2"x1⅜" pieces of metallic gold (Paper
    Pizazz™ Metallic Papers), one 3½"x4½" piece of ochre handmade, one
    5⅛"x8½" piece of brown, one 2⅝"x3⅝" piece of brown, two 2"x1½"
    pieces of brown
one 3"x4" piece of tan mat board
two 29¢ fishing lure stamps (each 1½"x1")
one 1¾" long brass feather charm (Creative Beginnings)
6½" of 1¾" wide brown satin/gold mesh ribbon
two 12" long strands of raffia
glue (see page 8)

1 Glue the alligator paper to the large piece of brown, then glue it
around the front, spine and back of the journal, starting ⅜" in
from the front right edge. Glue the ribbon vertically 1⅛" in from the
front right edge, wrapping the ends to the inside. Glue a 2"x1½"
brown piece to cover each ribbon end.

2 Fold the handmade paper ¼" from one long edge, moisten and tear. Glue to the center front. Glue the mat
board slightly to the left as shown. Glue the oatmeal paper to the center of the remaining brown piece, then to
the center of the mat board. Glue the stamps to the suede pieces, then to the gold pieces. Glue as shown. Loop the
raffia through the eye of the charm and fold in half; knot. Shred the raffia ends with your thumbnail. Glue to the
upper left of the stamps.

Americana Journal
by Becky Goughnour

one 9"x11" white spiral-bound journal (DMD Industries)
papers: one 1½"x2" piece of navy tiles (Paper Pizazz™ Bright Great Backgrounds), one 9"x12" piece of blue stars (Paper Pizazz™ Birthday Time), one 3½"x5" piece of navy checks, one 3½"x5" piece of navy tri-dot, one 3½"x5" piece of burgundy hearts, one 7" square of burgundy/white stripe, one 3"x2" piece of burgundy tri-dot (Paper Pizazz™ Dots, Checks, Plaids & Stripes)
burgundy cardstock: one 7¼" square, six 1⅝" squares
12" of ⅜" wide silver glitter self-adhesive ribbon
silver fine-tip pen, pencil, tracing paper, glue (see page 8)

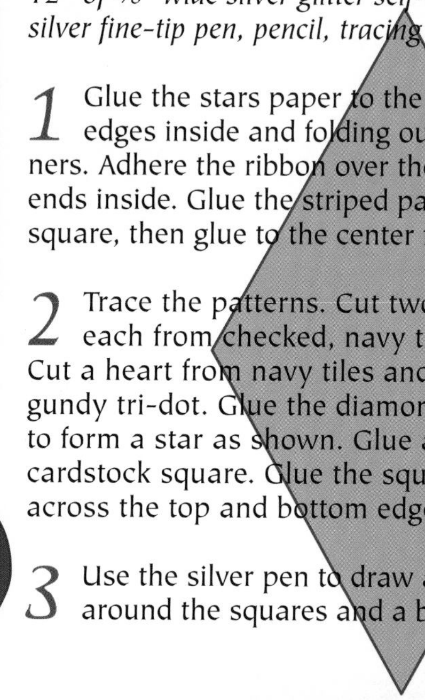

1 Glue the stars paper to the journal front, folding the edges inside and folding out the excess in the corners. Adhere the ribbon over the left edge, folding the ends inside. Glue the striped paper to the large cardstock square, then glue to the center front of the stars paper.

2 Trace the patterns. Cut two diamonds and a heart each from checked, navy tri-dot and heart paper. Cut a heart from navy tiles and two hearts from burgundy tri-dot. Glue the diamonds to the striped square to form a star as shown. Glue a heart to each small cardstock square. Glue the squares evenly spaced across the top and bottom edges of the journal front.

3 Use the silver pen to draw a ～～•～～• border around the squares and a bow above each heart.

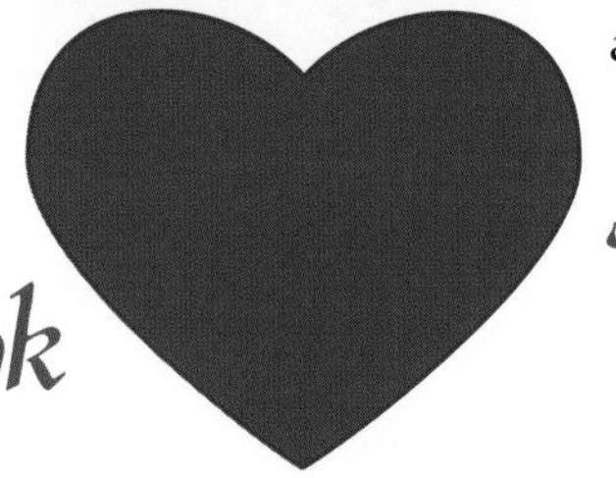

Little Fern Book

by Becky Goughnour

one 5"x7" white spiral-bound journal (Hiller)
papers: one 5¼"x8" piece of ferns, one 3⅝" square of bachelor's buttons (Paper Pizazz™ Floral Papers), one 2⅝" square of metallic gold (Paper Pizazz™ Metallic Papers)
black cardstock: one 4¾"x7" piece, one 3⅞" square
one 2⅜" square of dark green mat board
one 1⅜" tall square round floral letter sticker (Frances Meyer®)
9" of ⅜" wide blue grosgrain self-adhesive ribbon
decorative scissors (deckle by Family Treasures)
glue (see page 8)

1 Glue the large piece of black cardstock to the book front. Glue the ferns paper to cover the book front, leaving ⅛" of black showing on the binding edge. Glue the edges inside, folding out the excess in the corners. Adhere the ribbon ⅛" inside the left edge of the ferns paper.

2 Glue the bachelor's buttons paper to the remaining piece of cardstock, then to the book front, centered between the top and bottom edges and between the ribbon and the opening edge. Center the sticker on the mat board, then glue to the gold paper; trim with decorative scissors. Glue to the center of the bachelor's button square.

Hydrangeas & Cherub

by Katie Hacker

one 8"x6" brown corrugated spiral-bound journal
    (DMD Industries)
papers: one 1/2"x6" strip, one 1 1/2" square and one
    2" square of hydrangeas (Paper Pizazz™ Pretty
    Papers), one 5/8"x6" strip, one 1 5/8" square and
    one 2 1/8" square of metallic gold (Paper Pizazz™
    Metallic Papers), one 3/4"x6" strip, one 1 3/4"
    square and one 2 1/4" square of purple
one 1 1/2" wide brass cherub charm (Creative
    Beginnings)
three 10" lengths of 1/8" wide purple satin ribbon
glue (see page 8)

1 Glue the hydrangeas strip to the gold strip, then
   to the purple strip. Glue it 1/8" from the bound
edge of the journal front. Glue the 2" hydrangeas
square to the 2 1/8" gold square, then to the 2 1/4" purple square; glue diagonally to the center front of the
journal. Cut the remaining squares in half diagonally to make triangles. Layer and glue to the journal
corners as shown.

2 Glue the charm to the center of the center
   square. Hold the ribbons together and tie a
shoestring bow with 1 1/2" loops and 2 1/2" tails.
Glue above the charm.

Sunny Reflections

by Becky Goughnour

one 5 1/2"x8" corrugated journal (D&CC)
papers: one 4 3/4"x5 3/4" piece of green handmade-look, four
    1/4"x4 3/4" strips of cedar handmade-look (Paper Pizazz™
    Handmade Papers), two 1/4"x4 3/4" strips of brown swirl
    (Paper Pizazz™ Black & White Photos), one 2 1/2" square
    of metallic gold (Paper Pizazz™ Metallic Papers), one
    1/4"x4 3/4" strip and one 2 1/4" square of orange, one 2 3/8"
    square of yellow, one 2 5/8" square and one 4 3/4"x7 1/8" piece
    of brown, one 4 3/4"x7 1/8" piece of black, one 6"x7" piece of
    dark green handmade
twisted paper ribbon: four 1/2"x4 3/4" pieces of brown, two
    1/2"x4 3/4" pieces of ivory
two 4 3/4" lengths of 1/8" wide gold cord
sun stamp (RubberStampede®), black stamp pad
small handful of gold angel hair
decorative scissors (deckle by Family Treasures)
craft knife, metallic gold broad-tip pen, glue (see page 8)

1 Glue the black paper to the journal front. Crumple the
   large piece of brown into a ball, then smooth out and glue
to the black. Fold under 1/4" on each edge of the dark green
handmade, moisten and tear off. Glue diagonally on the
brown; tear the points flush with the book edge. Spread the
angel hair apart with your fingers and glue to the front,
extending over the edges of the journal. Make a gold dot on
each brown corner.

2 Use the knife to cut vertical slits 1/4" apart in the green
   handmade-look paper, leaving 1/4" uncut at the top and
bottom. Weave the 4 3/4" paper strips, paper ribbon lengths
and gold cord lengths through the slits, alternating as shown
(weave the gold lengths with the ivory paper ribbon lengths).
Glue the woven piece over the angel hair. Stamp the sun diagonally on the orange square. Glue to the yellow square, then
to the gold and brown squares. Trim the brown with the decorative scissors. Glue to the center of the woven piece.

Messenger of Peace

Paper Treasures & Holiday Pleasures

This chapter contains wonderful techniques to make Christmas decorations. A country-style wall hanging (page 106) welcomes friends into your home and shows your Christmas spirit. Tree decorations in romantic, whimsical, Victorian or country styles can adorn your tree in keeping with the style of your home décor.

The Christmas Wall Mats on page 106 are a great idea for sending a Christmas wish which combines the sentiment of a card with the appearance of a wall hanging. And, to top it off, this chapter offers a terrific design for a doily angel tree topper on page 108.

A few doilies, craft sticks, doll's hair yarn, or papier-mâché materials will go a long way in this chapter. The ideas and any instructions you'll need are provided in the following pages.

So gather your materials, stir up some Christmas cheer and get ready to have a handmade, homespun Merry Christmas!

Puffy Ornaments

by LeNae Gerig

for each ornament:
8" of 24-gauge wire, wire cutters
polyester fiberfill or cotton balls for stuffing
decorative scissors (mini scallop by Fiskars®)
black fine-tip pen, white paint pen
¹/₁₆" hole punch, needlenose pliers
tracing paper, pencil, glue (see page 8)

Trace the pattern, lay it on the folded brown paper and cut out two shapes. Refer to the project instructions to decorate one shape. Glue together around the outside edge, leaving a ½" opening; let dry. Trim with the decorative scissors. Stuff lightly with cotton balls and glue the opening closed. Punch holes as shown on the pattern. **Hanger:** Wrap the wire around the pencil to coil it; remove and stretch slightly. Insert the wire ends through the holes and use the pliers to twist them into "knots."

for the snowman:
papers: three ⁷/₈"x¹/₄" strips of green/white plaid
(Paper Pizazz™ Dots, Checks, Stripes & Plaids),
3½"x4" piece of brown kraft, one 2"
square of burgundy, one 1¹/₄"x¹/₄" piece
of black, one ³/₄"x³/₈" piece of black
one ½" wide burgundy button
two 1½" long twigs
heart punches: ³/₁₆", ¹/₄" (Family Treasures)

Draw the face with the black pen. Use the white pen to outline him with a wavy line and highlight his eyes. Glue the black papers to make his hat and the plaid papers to make his scarf as shown. Punch two ¹/₄" burgundy hearts and glue for his cheeks; punch two ³/₁₆" hearts and glue one to his hat and one for his heart. Leave space to insert the twig arms when gluing; after trimming the edges, glue the arms in place. Coil the wire, thread the button onto it and wrap the wire ends around his arms to attach.

for the heart:
papers: one ³/₄" square of green/white plaid (Paper Pizazz™ Dots, Checks,
Stripes & Plaids), ½" square red/white striped (Paper Pizazz™ Ho Ho
Ho!!!), 2½"x6" piece of brown kraft
one ½" wide navy blue button
9"x1" torn strip of green fabric with gold dots

Use the white pen to outline the heart with a wavy line. Glue the patterned papers as shown; use the black pen to draw stitches. Glue the button to the patches. Tie the fabric around the hanger, making a shoestring bow with 1¹/₄" loops and 1¹/₄" tails.

for the gingerbread man:
one 3½"x6" piece of brown paper
one 1" square of burgundy paper
heart punches: ³/₁₆", ¹/₄" (Family Treasures)
one ⁵/₈" wide green button
fine-tip pens: green, red

Draw the face with the black pen. Punch two ¹/₄" burgundy hearts and glue for his cheeks; punch two ³/₁₆" ones and glue for buttons. Use the white pen to outline him with a wavy line and highlight his eyes. Draw a wavy green line across each wrist and ankle; repeat with red. Thread the button onto the wire after coiling it, then attach it to the ornament.

Tree Box
by Becky Goughnour

one 8"x6"x2" wood box with a hinged lid and a removable
   insert for placing a photo
papers: one 12" square of holly (Paper Pizazz™ Ho Ho
   Ho!!!), one 4½"x6¼" piece of red moiré (Paper Pizazz™
   Black & White Photos), three ⅜"x11" strips of metallic
   gold (Paper Pizazz™ Metallic Papers)
Christmas tree, holly garland stickers (The Gifted Line®)
acrylic paints: metallic gold, dark green
matte acrylic wood sealer
one 1" wide paintbrush, small sea sponge
sandpaper, clean cloth, newspapers
Phillips head screwdriver
glue (see page 8)

1 Protect your work surface with newspapers. Use
   the screwdriver to remove the hinges and clasps
from the box. Remove the wood insert and plastic
from the lid. Sand the box lightly and clean with the
cloth. Apply a coat of sealer; let dry. Use the paint-
brush to apply two coats of gold to the inside of the box and the lid; let dry.

2 Wet the sponge and blot on the newspapers. Dip in green paint, dab excess onto the newspapers, then sponge
   the lid, allowing gold to show through. Let dry, then seal again.

3 Cut two 7"x2" and two 9"x2" strips of holly paper. Cover each short box side with glue, then press on a 7"x2"
   strip of holly paper. Align the top edges with the box edge; fold the ends around the corners and the bottom
edges under the box. Repeat with 8"x2" strips to cover the long sides; trim the paper even on the ends. Cut a 6"x8"
piece of holly paper and glue it to the box bottom. Glue the gold strips around the top edge.

4 Place the holly garland stickers around the top of the lid, framing the
   open area. Center the tree sticker on the moiré paper. Reassemble
the box, placing the moiré paper under the plastic.

Heart Ornament
by Sandy Bunka

one 2½"x2½"x1" papier-mâché puffy heart with a 2" long gold thread hanger
one 12" square of burgundy/peach patterned tissue paper
9" of 1" wide white sheer ribbon with gold wired edges
one 1" wide brass heart charm
one 6mm (³/₁₆") purple acrylic rhinestone
one 2" long ivory tassel with a gold bell cap and chain
gold acrylic paint
one ½" wide flat paintbrush, small sea sponge
decoupage glue, glue (see page 8)

1 Tear the tissue into 1" pieces. Use decoupage glue to attach the
   squares to the heart, overlapping as needed to cover; let dry.
Sponge lightly with gold paint; let dry.

2 Glue the charm to one side of the heart. Spread the bell cap and
   glue to the point of the heart. Use the ribbon to make a shoestring
bow with 1" loops and 2" tails; glue to the top of the heart.

Christmas Wall Cards
by Sandy Bunka

for each card:
one 5½"x7" piece of green mat board
one 5½"x⅜" heart/circle strip rub-on decal
black pens: broad-tip, fine-tip
white paint pen, glitter glue pen, glue (see page 8)
Believe! card:
one 2½"x4¼" Santa rub-on decal
1 yard of ¼" wide green/red/white cord
two ⅞" wide wood stars
four ½" wide metallic gold confetti stars
dark yellow acrylic paint, #4 flat paintbrush
Merry Christmas card:
rub-on decals: one 1¾"x4" reindeer, one ½"x4" star/heart
   strip, one additional 5½"x⅜" heart/circle strip
four 2" long green PVC pine sprigs
two 1" long sprigs of ¼"−⅜" wide pink artificial berries
1 yard of ¼" wide green/gold cord

1 Follow the manufacturer's directions to apply decals to the mat board as shown. Use a white pen to draw dots and snowflakes around them. Dot glitter into each snowflake center. Cut a 27½" and a 5½" cord length. Glue the 5½" length to the top. Glue the 27½" length from one lower corner up the long side. Loop 8" over the top for a hanger, then glue the rest down the other side and across the base.

2 **Believe! card:** Use the broad pen to write "Believe!" above Santa and the fine pen to draw dashes along each letter. Paint the stars yellow. Glue a confetti star to the center of each, then use the thin pen to draw a dashed border. Glue a wood star to each upper corner with a confetti star beside it. **Merry Christmas card:** Use the broad pen to write "Merry Christmas" at the top; add dashes as before. Glue two pine sprigs and a berry sprig to each top corner.

Happy Holidays Hanging
by Katie Hacker

corrugated cardboard: one 10¼"x3½" piece of brown, one 1" square of burgundy, four ½"x1" strips of white, one 1" square of dark green (MPR Paperbilities™)
one 4"x2½" piece of white cardstock
die cuts: one 5¼" long blue corrugated mitten, one 3" long green corrugated holly leaf with red berries, one 4½" wide yellow corrugated star (Accu/Cut® Systems) (or use the patterns on page 141 to cut from corrugated cardboard)
1¼" die-cut red corrugated alphabet letters "HAPPY HOLIDAYS" (Accu/Cut® Systems)
punches: ⅞" star corner rounder (Family Treasures), ¼" round (McGill, Inc.)
4" tall oval template, pencil, fine-tip black pen
18-gauge black wire: three 6" lengths, one 15" length
18" of jute twine, glue (see page 8)

1 Use the star corner punch on each corner of the 10¼" cardboard and to cut a dark green star. Punch four ¼" burgundy circles. Cut an oval from cardstock. Use the pen to make a dashed border around the oval and each corrugated piece. Glue the holly and berries to the oval and the white strips to the mitten cuff. Trim the strips even with the cuff, then glue a circle to each white strip. Glue the green star to the yellow star center. Glue the letters to the brown cardboard as shown.

2 Wrap each wire length loosely around a pencil to coil it, then remove and stretch slightly. Poke one end of a 6" length through the star; bend the end up to secure. Insert the other end into the bottom left of the brown cardboard and bend the end down. Repeat to attach the oval and the mitten as shown. Poke the ends of the 15" length through the top of the sign to make a hanger. Knot a 2" length of jute around each 6" wire length. Tie the remaining jute around the hanger, making a shoestring bow with 1½" loops and 3" tails.

Angel Topiaries

by Sandy Bunka

for each topiary:

one 5"–6" long cinnamon stick
metallic gold acrylic paint
one ½" wide paintbrush
small sea sponge
decorative scissors (pinking, heartbeat by
   Fiskars®)
iron, ironing board
polyester fiberfill
one 2"x3" piece of floral foam for silks and
   drieds
serrated knife
½ oz. of Spanish moss
½ oz. of assorted dried materials
glue (see page 8)

trumpeter angel:

one 3" wide terra cotta pot
one 6"x3" piece of trumpeting angel fabric
one 6"x3" piece of fusible webbing
two 7"x4" pieces of brown kraft paper
10" of ⅝" wide gold pearl drop trim
10" of ½" wide burgundy/green gimp braid
10" of 1" wide burgundy/white fabric ribbon
burgundy acrylic paint

star angel:

one 2½" wide terra cotta pot
one 3½"x4" piece of angel fabric
one 3½"x4" piece of fusible webbing
two 4½"x5" pieces of brown kraft paper
one 10" long sprig of green PVC pine
10" of 1" wide burgundy/black fabric ribbon
six 24" long strands of raffia
one 1¼" wide wood star, one ½" wide gold jingle bell
black fine-tip permanent pen, yellow acrylic paint

1 **Base:** Paint the pot gold; let dry. Trim the foam to fit into the pot and glue in place. Insert the cinnamon stick into the foam, then remove and set aside for step 2. Glue Spanish moss to cover the top of the foam.

2 **For either angel:** Follow the manufacturer's instructions to fuse webbing to the back of the fabric, then cut out with pinking shears. Sponge one side of each paper piece with gold paint; sponge the edges with acrylic paint (burgundy for the trumpeter angel, yellow for the star angel). Peel the backing paper from the fused fabric and fuse to the center of one piece of paper. Glue the pieces together close to the edges; leave a 1" opening at the bottom. Trim the paper edges with heartbeat scissors. Highlight selected areas with glitter glue. Lightly stuff the angel, then glue the cinnamon stick into the opening. Glue the other end into the hole in the foam.

3 **Trumpeter angel:** Glue gimp around the pot rim with the pearl trim over it. Use the ribbon to make a shoe-string bow with 1½" loops and 2" tails. Trim the tails with the pinking shears. Glue to the bottom front of the cinnamon stick. Cut the dried materials into 1" sprigs and glue around the base of the cinnamon and into the bow center as shown.

4 **Star angel:** Glue the pine sprig around the pot rim. Paint the star yellow and glue to the topiary top. Use the pen to make a —•— border around the fabric and the star. Hold the raffia together and make a shoestring bow with 2" loops and 9" tails; glue behind the star. Glue the bell to the center of the her bow. Cut the dried materials into 1" sprigs and glue around the base of the cinnamon and into the bow center as shown.

Angel Hanging

by Marilyn Gossett

wood: 2 jumbo craft sticks, three 2" long ovals, two
   1 1/4" long ovals, one 1 1/4" circle, one 1/2"x1" rectangle
round white paper doilies: one 4", two 8"
blonde Lil' Loopies doll hair (One & Only Creations®)
three 10" lengths of 1/16" wide metallic gold shredded
   ribbon
one 3/8" wide blue oval acrylic rhinestone
one 3/4" wide gold plastic ring
acrylic paints: pale peach, white, black, metallic gold,
   dark pink
dimensional paint: metallic gold
round wood toothpick, small sea sponge
one 1/4" wide flat paintbrush
wire cutters, needlenose pliers, drill with 1/16" bit
24-gauge gold wire: one 6" length, one 12" length
glue (see page 8)

1 **Body:** Refer to the diagram on page 143 to glue the wood pieces together. Paint the face, hands and legs peach, the sleeves and socks white and the shoes black. Paint the cheeks pink; use the toothpick to dot white cheek highlights and black eyes. Make gold dots on the sleeves and shoes.

2 **Banner:** Paint the remaining craft stick white. Sponge gold around the edges; let dry. Use the black pen to write "Messenger of Peace" in the center. Use the paintbrush handle to dot metallic gold spots randomly around the edges. Drill holes in each upper corner, the lower center and the top of the angel's head. Wrap each wire length around the paintbrush handle to coil it. Thread the ends of the short length through the holes to connect the banner and body. Thread the ends of the long length through both upper holes to make a hanger.

3 **Dress & wings:** Sponge gold around the doily edges; let dry. Cut each 8" doily in half and fold into 1/2" pleats. Glue a piece to the front and one to the back, matching the cut edges. Fold the 4" doily in half, cut from one side to the fold and glue around the neck with the cut in the back. Glue the remaining doily halves for wings. Wrap a strand of hair around your hand 40 times, tie in the middle with a 4" length and glue to the head. Glue the ring for a halo.

4 Apply a large dot of dimensional paint to the collar. Gently press the rhinestone into the paint; let dry. Hold the ribbon lengths together and tie in a shoestring bow with 1" loops and 3" tails; glue above the rhinestone.

Angel Tree Topper

by Marilyn Gossett

one 6"x10" piece of blue velour posterboard (MPR Associates, Inc.)
doilies: one 6" wide metallic gold heart, one 4" wide metallic gold
   heart, one 6" round white, two 8" round white, one 1" round
   metallic gold
wood: two 1" long teardrops, one 1 1/4" circle
two 3" lengths of wavy white doll hair
one 3/8" wide oval purple acrylic rhinestone
acrylic paints: black, white
metallic gold dimensional paint
pink powdered blush, cotton swab, round wood toothpick
tracing paper, pencil
glue (see page 8)

1 Trace the pattern and cut from posterboard. Overlap and glue the edges to form a cone. Cut each 8" doily in half and fold into 1/2" pleats. Glue the pleated pieces to the front, back and sides of the cone. **Arms:** Cut a 3/4"x9" strip of posterboard and fold in half, velour sides together. Cut the 6" white doily in half and pleat each half as before. Glue the straight edge of each pleated doily between the posterboard layers just below the fold, extending opposite directions to form a T. Glue a teardrop at each end for hands.

2 Glue the arms into the cone. Pinch the rounded edges of the 4" gold heart doily and glue for a bodice. **Head:** Blush the cheeks of the wood circle. Dip the toothpick in black paint and dot eyes. Highlight each cheek with a white dot. Fluff the hair and glue to the head as shown. Glue the 1" doily for a halo. Glue the head to the top of the bodice. Glue the 6" heart doily for wings. Apply a dot of dimensional paint to the bodice center. Gently press the rhinestone into the paint; let dry.

Heart Ornament

by Sandy Bunka

one 3 1/2"x4 1/4"x 1/4"
    papier-mâché heart
Christmas stickers (Suzy's Zoo®)
white acrylic paint
fine-tip pens: black, red
broad-tip pens: red, blue
glitter glue pen
matte acrylic spray sealer

back view

1 Seal the heart; paint white; let dry. Use the broad red pen to draw a ▬ ▬ border around the outer edge and a ▬ • ▬ border around one side. Use the blue and fine red pens to draw a ▬ • ▬ border around the other side.

2 Apply stickers to the center of each side as shown. Use the black pen to draw snow-flakes on one side. Add glitter glue to selected areas. Seal; let dry.

Snowflake Ornament

by Caryl McHarney

one 4 1/2"x6 1/4" snowflake card (Cards with Pizazz)
9" of metallic gold cord
tracing paper, ruler, stylus or embossing tool
1/16" hole punch, glue (see page 8)

Trace the pattern. Cut the card in half and trace the pattern onto the back of each piece. Cut out and score along the fold lines. Punch holes as shown on the top card half only. Fold into a pyramid, turning the half circles outward; glue the flaps inside the straight edges. Glue the top and bottom pyramids together at the half circles. Thread the cord through the holes at the top and knot the ends together for a hanger.

Fan Ornaments

by Katie Hacker

for each ornament:
glue (see page 8)
for the aqua ornament:
one 7 1/2"3 3/4" piece of aqua/pink swirl paper (Paper Pizazz™ Light Great Backgrounds)
one 7 1/2" long purple tassel loop with a 2 1/2" long tassel
one 5"x3" brunette angel with purple wings (Artifacts Inc.)
for the pink ornament:
one 10 1/2"x3" piece of pink rosebuds paper (Paper Pizazz™ Floral Papers)
one 10 1/2"x2 1/4" piece of laser lace paper (Paper Pizazz™ Romantic Papers)
one 7 1/2" long pink tassel loop with a 2 1/2" long tassel
one 1 1/2"x2 1/2" angel with a rose basket (Artifacts Inc.)
decorative scissors (colonial by Fiskars®)

1 **Aqua ornament:** Fold the paper widthwise into 1/2" pleats. Glue the cord of the tassel into the back of the first and last pleats so the the tassel hangs below the fan and the cord loops above for a hanger. Glue the lower 1/2" of the folds together. Glue the angel to the front as shown.

2 **Pink ornament:** Glue the laser lace to the bottom edge of the rosebuds paper, then use the decorative scissors to trim the top edge. Follow step 1 to complete the ornament.

Mom

For You

Love

Gifts, Presents & Splendid Surprises

Let the designs offered in this chapter inspire you with new gift-giving ideas. From bookmarks to jewelry and many things in between, this section shows how to make all sorts of practical and elegant gifts.

The sachet pockets on page 112 are as scent-sational as the perfumed materials inside them. The bookmarks (page 119) are simple enough for a child to create, making them a great gift for anyone from grandmothers to friends at school. Depending on the papers or embellishments you choose, they can be elegant, whimsical, inspiring or just downright silly! Pocket cards (see pages 114–115) are sentimental gifts that include an added surprise. You can tailor each to please the recipient you have in mind.

A bit of thread and a needle, some paper, ribbons, buttons, and, of course, scissors and glue are most of what you'll need to finish the crafts offered here. This chapter will show how to combine these materials to create gifts made from love.

Seed Packet Sachets by Marilyn Gossett

for each sachet:
7"x6" piece of paper
glue (see page 8)
tracing paper, pencil, ruler
2 Tbsp. of potpourri

Trace the pattern. Lay it on the back of the paper and trace around the outline. Use the ruler to lightly pencil lines connecting the inside corners, as shown by the dashed lines on the pattern. Cut out.

Fold the right flap in, then fold the left side over and glue in place. Fold up and glue the bottom flap. Fill with potpourri, fold the top flap down and glue. Embellish as shown in the project photo.

Lavender Heart Sachet

sachet made from purple swirl paper
papers: one 2"x2¹⁄₂" piece of purple swirl (Paper Pizazz™ Pretty Papers), one 2"x3" piece and one 1"x10" strip of purple handmade-look (Paper Pizazz™ Handmade Papers), 1"x2" piece of burgundy mulberry paper
one ³⁄₈" wide lavender ribbon rose with ribbon leaves
one ¹⁄₂" wide brass open heart charm
10" of ¹⁄₂" wide purple satin picot ribbon
decorative scissors (wave by Family Treasures, bow tie by Fiskars®)

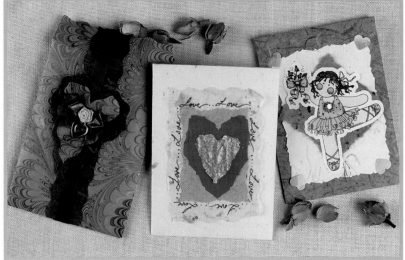

Love Heart Sachet

sachet made from ivory handmade paper
one 2¹⁄₂"x4" piece of ivory rice paper. one 2"x3" piece of tan handmade paper, one 2"x3" piece of red tissue paper, one 1¹⁄₂" square of metallic gold crinkle paper
dark red fine-tip pen
decorative scissors (bow tie by Fiskars®)

Ballerina Sachet

sachet made from turquoise handmade-look paper (Paper Pizazz™)
papers: one 1¹⁄₂" square of pink roses (Paper Pizazz™ Holidays & Seasons), one 3"x4" piece of ivory handmade paper with tinsel, one 2¹⁄₂" square of mauve handmade tissue paper
one 3" tall ballerina (Paper Pizazz™ Punch-Outs™ for Cards)
¹⁄₂" heart punch (Family Treasures)
one ¹⁄₄" wide clear acrylic rhinestone in gold setting
decorative scissors (bow tie by Fiskars®)

Vellum Fern Sachet

sachet made from fern paper and vellum (Paper Pizazz™)
one 2¹⁄₂"x3" piece of fern paper (Paper Pizazz™ Floral Papers)
one 3³⁄₈" long rose (Paper Pizazz™ Punch-Outs⁻¹ for Cards)
two ³⁄₁₆" wide clear acrylic rhinestones
two 9" lengths of gold thread
two 9" long strands of of raffia
2³⁄₄" wide heart template

Lay the vellum over the fern paper and handle as if they were one piece.

Pink Rose Sachet

sachet made from pink lace paper (Paper Pizazz™ Pretty Papers)
papers: one 2"x3" piece of metallic gold crinkle, one 1¹⁄₂"x2" piece of green mulberry paper
one 1" wide pink organza rose with leaf
one 6mm (¹⁄₄") clear acrylic rhinestone
decorative scissors (bow tie by Fiskars®)

Quilt Sachet

sachet made from Irish chain quilt paper (Paper Pizazz™ Country)
papers: one 2"x3" piece of metallic gold (Hygloss), one 1" square of metallic gold crinkle, one 1¹⁄₂" square of burgundy mulberry paper
one ³⁄₄" wide pink button
four 12" long strands of raffia
decorative scissors (wave by Family Treasures)

Use the decorative scissors to cut ¹⁄₄" wide strips of the smooth gold paper.

Flower Girl Hangers
by Marilyn Gossett

for each hanger:
1 jumbo craft stick (arms), one 1¼" wood circle (face)
acrylic paints: pale peach, peach, black, white, green
½" wide flat paintbrush, drill with 1/16" bit
1 yard of 24-gauge gold wire, needlenose pliers
glue (see page 8)

for the pink flower girl:
one 5" circle of pink roses paper (Paper Pizazz™ Wedding)
decorative scissors (bow tie by Fiskars®)
wood circles: two 1¼", two ¾", two ⅜"
four ¾" long wood teardrops, one 2" long wood oval
acrylic paints: pink, yellow
clear Dimensional Magic™ sealer (Plaid Enterprises, Inc.)
round white doilies: one 3", one 6"
blonde Lil' Loopies™ doll hair (One & Only Creations®)

for the purple flower girl:
one 5" circle of purple hydrangeas paper (Paper Pizazz™ Pretty
   Papers)
decorative scissors (wave by Family Treasures)
acrylic paints: purple, lavender, yellow
clear Dimensional Magic™ sealer (Plaid Enterprises, Inc.)
blonde Lil' Loopies™ doll hair (One & Only Creations®)
4" round white doily

for the angel:
paper doilies: two 6" round white, one 4" metallic gold heart
one 5" square of metallic gold foil board (Hygloss)
one 1" wide pink ribbon carnation with green leaves
12" of metallic gold shredded ribbon
6" of blonde Raf-A-Doodles doll hair (One & Only Creations®)
decorative scissors (scallop by Fiskars®)
4" of 20-gauge gold wire

1 Pink flower girl: Drill a hole in each end of the craft stick. Paint the craft stick and one 1¼" circle pale peach. Dot black eyes. Paint the cheeks peach, then dot with white highlights. Lay flat and apply sealer following the manufacturer's instructions; let dry.

2 Hat: Cut the remaining 1¼" circle in half (save one half for another project). Glue to the back of the 2" oval, straight edge down. Paint pink. *Flowers:* Paint the ¾" circles pink, the ⅜" circles yellow with white highlights and the teardrops green. Glue the flowers together as shown, then use the pen to squiggle irregular outlines around the hat, flowers and leaves.

3 Trim the paper circle with the decorative scissors. Fold it and the 6" doily in half. Glue the paper circle over the craft stick and the doily to the back. Fold a ½" box pleat (see diagram) in the center of the 3" doily. Fold the top ⅓ over the craft stick. Glue the head to the top center; glue the hat to the back of her head. Glue one flower to the hat and one below her chin. *Hair:* Cut a ¼" thick hank to 6" long and knot in the middle. Glue the knot to the top front of the head as shown.

4 Hanger: Coil the wire around a pencil or the paintbrush handle; remove. Poke one wire end through the hole on each end of the craft stick, back to front. Use the pliers to twist the wire ends into a tight coil.

5 Purple flower girl: Follow steps 1–4; paint the flowers purple and the flower centers and hat lavender; highlight with yellow dots. Omit the 6" doily. *Hair:* Coil each side; glue to secure.

6 Angel: Follow step 1 above for the face and arms, omitting the sealer. Fold a 1" box pleat in one 6" doily and glue over the craft stick. Cut a 1" border off the other doily, fold into ½" pleats and glue under her chin. Shape the 4" wire into a circle, twist the ends and glue for a halo. *Wings:* Glue the heart doily to the foil board and trim with decorative scissors. Glue to her back. Glue on the hair. Glue the shredded ribbon and carnation below her chin. Follow step 4 for the hanger.

Pockets Full of Love

by Marilyn Gossett

Follow step 2 on page 16 to make the pockets, using the 8½" paper square from the project supply list, but lay the card on the diagonal paper square to determine the placements for the folds.

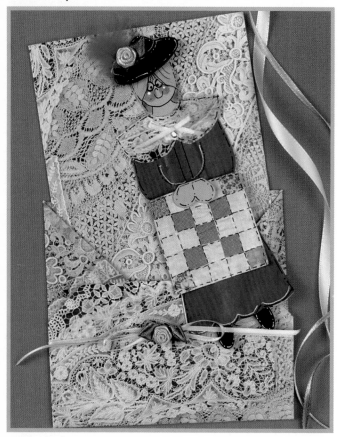

Heartstrings

one 4½"x6¼" purple swirl card (Cards with Pizazz)
papers: one 8½" square of antique lace (Paper Pizazz™ Black & White Photos), one 8½"x4" piece and one 2" square of Irish chain quilt (Paper Pizazz™ Country)
one "Families are tied together with heart strings" plaque (Paper Pizazz Sayings Punch-Outs™)
two ½" wide pink silk flowers
one ⅜" wide brass double heart charm
wood: 1 craft spoon, one 1½" square, one 1½" oval, one ⅞" heart, two ⅞" teardrops
acrylic paints: pale peach, peach, medium brown, white
matte acrylic sealer, #2 flat paintbrush
black fine-tip permanent pen, craft saw or tinsnips
tracing paper, transfer paper, pencil, glue (see page 8)

Follow step 1 above, but make the hair, hat and feet brown (patterns on page 141). Paint white cuffs on the cut edge of the hands. Use the quilt paper and the pattern to make the dress. Follow step 2 to assemble her; refer to the photo for embellishments. Glue the saying to the front of the pocket. Insert the card and figure into the pocket.

Quilting Grandma

papers: one 8½" square and one 2½"x1½" piece of antique lace, one 5" square of purple moiré, one 2" square of Irish chain quilt (Paper Pizazz™)
one 4½"x6¼" antique lace card (Cards with Pizazz)
one 1½" long violet feather
two ⅜" wide lavender ribbon roses
one 4mm (⅛") clear acrylic rhinestone
1 yard of ⅛" wide ivory satin ribbon
wood: 1 craft spoon, one 1½" square, one 1½" oval, one ⅞" heart, two ⅞" teardrops
acrylic paints: pale peach, peach, gray, medium brown, black, white
matte acrylic sealer, #2 flat paintbrush, #00 liner paintbrush
black fine-tip permanent pen, craft saw or tinsnips
tracing paper, transfer paper, pencil, glue (see page 8)

collar (trace on fold)

brim

hands

1. Transfer the face pattern to the spoon; paint as shown. Cut the point off the heart, then paint it pale peach; paint the oval and teardrops black. Use the pen to draw the black details and the liner brush with white to paint the white details. Let dry; seal.

shoe

2. **Dress:** Trace the pattern onto folded tracing paper; unfold. Cut two from purple paper. Use the black pen and white paint to make the details. Glue one to each side of the spoon, front sides out. Glue the points of the teardrops to the bottom between the layers. Cut a collar from lace paper and glue in place; glue the quilt paper over the wood square. Use the pen to draw stitches on both. Glue the quilt to the front of the dress; glue the heart over it for hands. Glue the black oval for the hat brim. Glue the feather and rose to the hat as shown. Use a 9" ribbon length to make a

shoestring bow with ½" loops and 1" tails; glue below her chin. Glue the rhinestone below the bow.

3. Insert the card and Grandma into the pocket. Tie the remaining ribbon around the pocket, making a shoestring bow with 1" loops and 2" tails. Glue the last rose to the bow center.

Window Cards with Sachets

Follow the instructions on page 112 to make the sachets, using the 7"x6" piece of paper from the project supply list. Slip the sachet inside the card before placing the card in the pocket.

for each card:
glue (see page 8), tracing paper, pencil, ruler
craft knife, cutting mat
2 Tbsp. of potpourri (for sachet)

for the corrugated card:
sachet: one 7"x6" piece of yellow daisies paper (Paper Pizazz™ Floral Papers)
pocket: one 8½" square of ivy paper (Paper Pizazz™)
one 4½"x6¼" brown corrugated card (Cards with Pizazz)
4½" tall diamond template, 3½"x5" piece of acetate
½" heart punch (Family Treasures)
double-stick tape, five 36" long strands of raffia

for the lace card:
sachet: one 7"x6" piece of white rosebuds paper (Paper Pizazz™ Floral Papers)
pocket: one 8½" square of oatmeal handmade-look paper (Paper Pizazz™ Solid Muted Colors)
one 8½"x2½" strip of laser lace paper (Paper Pizazz™)
one 4½"x6¼" diagonal lace card (Cards with Pizazz)
3¾" tall oval template, 3½"x5" piece of acetate
double-stick tape
two 18" lengths of ivory satin ribbon
one ⅜" wide white ribbon rosebud with ribbon leaves

for the heart card:
sachet: one 7"x6" piece of azaleas paper (Paper Pizazz™ Floral Papers)
pocket: one 8½" square of pink moiré paper (Paper Pizazz™ Wedding)
one 4½"x6¼" green marble card (Cards with Pizazz)
corner edger (nostalgia by Fiskars®), 4" tall heart template
metallic gold paint pen, ¼" hole punch (McGill, Inc.)
1 yard of ¼" wide metallic gold grosgrain ribbon

1 **Corrugated card:** Trace the template on the inside front of the card; cut out. Tape the acetate over the inside of the window. From the scraps of yellow paper left from the sachet, punch four hearts. Glue to the card front with the points at the window corners. Use the ivy paper to make a pocket. Tie with the raffia, making a shoestring bow with 2" loops and 8" tails.

2 **Lace card:** Follow step 1 to cut and line the window. Use oatmeal paper to make a pocket; cut out the lace and glue around the pocket. Hold both ribbon lengths together and wrap around the pocket, knotting in the front. Glue the rose to the knot.

3 **Heart card:** Follow step 1 to cut the window. Use the pen to draw a wavy line around the window. Edge the card corners, then punch three holes diagonally, ½" apart, in the top right corner. Weave an 8" ribbon length through the holes and knot at the top. Use the moiré paper to make a pocket; use the edger on the front flap corners. Embellish with the pen as shown. Tie the remaining ribbon around the pocket, making a shoestring bow with 1½" loops and 2" tails.

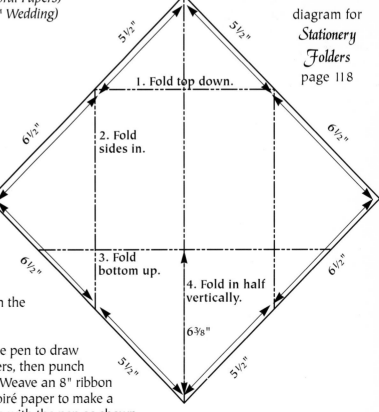

diagram for
Stationery Folders
page 118

5½" 5½"
6½" 6½"

1. Fold top down.

2. Fold sides in.

6½" 6½"

3. Fold bottom up.

4. Fold in half vertically.

6⅜"

5½" 5½"

Stuffed Paper Ornaments
by Marilyn Gossett

"Quilted" Angel

papers: one 8"x6" piece of pink lace (Paper Pizazz™),
   one 10"x8½" piece of Irish chain quilt (Paper Pizazz™
   Country)
acrylic paints: pale peach, peach, black, white, medium
   brown
matte acrylic sealer, ½" wide flat paintbrush
6" of ¼" wide metallic gold ribbon
9" of ¼" wide mauve satin ribbon
eight 12" long strands of raffia
one 4" round white paper doily
two ⅝" wide brown buttons
1 yard of 24-gauge gold wire, needlenose pliers
blonde Lil' Loopies™ doll hair (One & Only Creations®)
black fine-tip permanent pen, white paint pen
polyester fiberfill
tracing paper, transfer paper, pencil, glue (see page 8)

1   Trace the wing and body patterns from page 117
   onto folded tracing paper; unfold. Cut two angels
from quilt paper and two wings from lace. Transfer the
face, hand and foot patterns to one body piece; paint
as shown. Use the black pen to draw the mouth and to
make stitching lines around the wings and around all
the light areas of the body. Use the white pen to divide
the shoes and make stitching lines around them.

2   Thin brown paint with an equal amount of water.
   Use the flat brush to lightly shade the sleeve and
dress edges and around each leg. Let dry, then use
the sealer for a satiny gloss. **Body:** Glue the front
and back edges, back sides together, leaving the top
of the head open; let dry. Stuff softly, then glue the
head closed.

3   Glue on the hair. Glue the ends of the
   gold ribbon together, forming a circle;
glue to the hair for a halo. Fold a 1" box
pleat in the doily center (see diagram), fold
under 1½" on the top and glue for a collar, turning
the ends to the back over the sleeves. Glue a button
to the bottom collar and one to the dress below the
collar. Use the ribbon to make a shoestring bow with
½" loops and 1" tails; glue to the collar top. Hold the
raffia together and tie in a shoestring bow with 1"
loops and 5" tails; glue under the ribbon bow.

4   **Wings:** Glue the edges, back sides together; let
   dry. Cut a slit in the center front and stuff softly,
then glue the opening closed. Coil the wire around the
pencil; remove. Poke one wire end through each side
of the wings, back to front, at the point marked with
the black dot. Using the pliers, twist the wire ends to
keep them from pulling out. Glue the wings to the
upper body back.

Apple for Teacher

one 7"x10" piece of red paper with white dots (Paper Pizazz™ Ho
   Ho Ho!!!)
acrylic paints: brown, black, green
matte acrylic sealer, ½" wide flat paintbrush
black fine-tip permanent pen, white paint pen
six 12" long strands of raffia
1 yard of 24-gauge gold wire, needle-nose pliers
polyester fiberfill
tracing paper
transfer paper
pencil
glue (see page 8)

(The pattern is
on page 117.) A
stuffed apple
with painted
details is simple
to make and is
a great gift for
your favorite
teacher—or
personalize it
for a child's first
year in school.

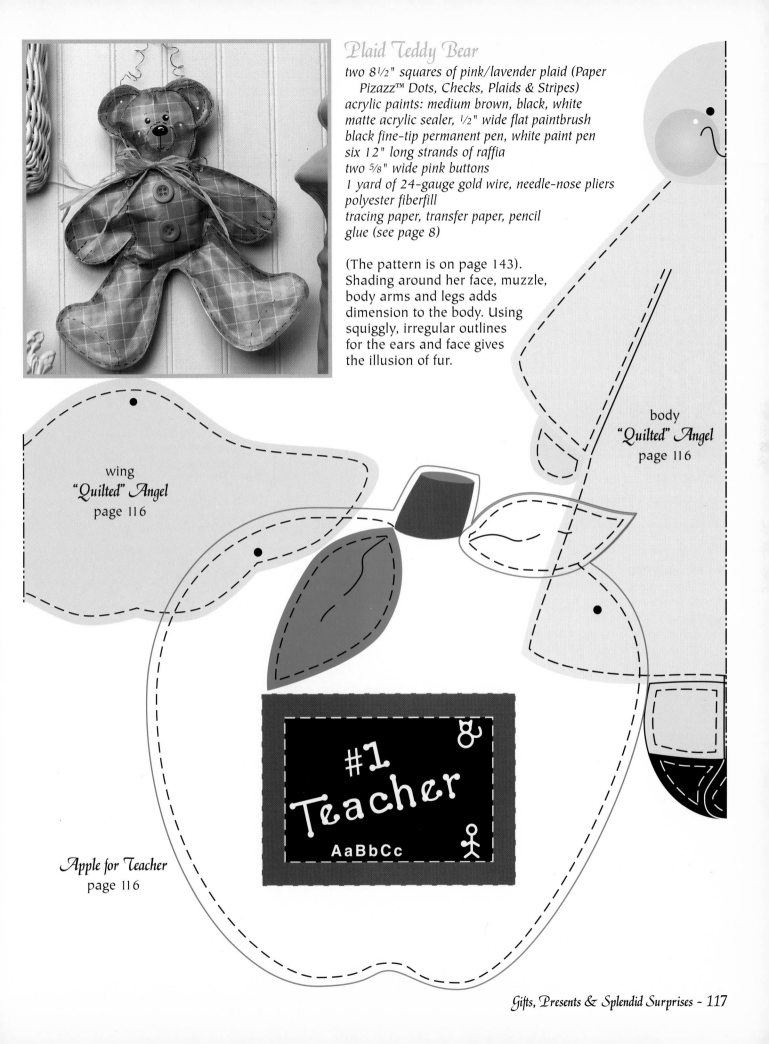

Plaid Teddy Bear

two 8½" squares of pink/lavender plaid (Paper Pizazz™ Dots, Checks, Plaids & Stripes)
acrylic paints: medium brown, black, white
matte acrylic sealer, ½" wide flat paintbrush
black fine-tip permanent pen, white paint pen
six 12" long strands of raffia
two ⅝" wide pink buttons
1 yard of 24-gauge gold wire, needle-nose pliers
polyester fiberfill
tracing paper, transfer paper, pencil
glue (see page 8)

(The pattern is on page 143). Shading around her face, muzzle, body arms and legs adds dimension to the body. Using squiggly, irregular outlines for the ears and face gives the illusion of fur.

wing
"Quilted" Angel
page 116

body
"Quilted" Angel
page 116

Apple for Teacher
page 116

#1 Teacher

AaBbCc

Stationery Packets

by Marilyn Gossett

Dress up a traditional gift of stationery with a creatively-tied folder. We used ready-made cards and envelopes, but you can make this present even more special by crafting handmade stationery.

Pink Roses Folder

one 12" square of pink roses paper (Paper Pizazz™ Wedding)
6 pink roses cards, 6 white envelopes (Cards with Pizazz)
one ¾" wide wood heart button
acrylic paints: pink, ivory
#2 flat paintbrush, black fine-tip permanent pen
five 24" long strands of raffia
clear Dimensional Magic™ sealer (Plaid Enterprises, Inc.), glue (see page 8)

Follow the diagram on page 115 to make the 12" paper square into a folder. Place the cards in the front pocket and the envelopes in the back pocket. Tie with the raffia, making a shoestring bow with 1½" loops and 5" tails. Paint the heart pink; let dry. Paint an ivory "stitch" between the holes. Use the pen to outline with dots and squiggles. Follow the manufacturer's instructions to seal; let dry. Glue the heart to the bow center.

Flowers & Lace

one 12" square of diagonal trims paper (Paper Pizazz™)
6 purple hydrangeas cards, 6 white envelopes (Cards with Pizazz)
1 yard of ⅜" wide pink satin picot ribbon
1½" sprig of ½" wide purple silk flowers, glue (see page 8)

Holly Folder

one 12" square of holly paper (Paper Pizazz™)
6 red plaid cards, 6 green envelopes (Cards with Pizazz™)
one ⅝" wide wood star
acrylic paints: gold, white
#2 flat paintbrush, black fine-tip permanent pen
clear Dimensional Magic™ (Plaid Enterprises, Inc.)
five 24" long strands of raffia, glue (see page 8)

Plaid & Gingerbread

12" square of red/white plaid paper (Paper Pizazz™)
6 gingerbread cards, 6 white envelopes (Cards with Pizazz)
two 1" wide wood heart buttons
acrylic paints: red, white
#2 flat paintbrush, black fine-tip permanent pen
clear Dimensional Magic™ (Plaid Enterprises, Inc.)
five 24" long strands of raffia, glue (see page 8)

Pine & Lights

one 12" square of pine boughs paper (Paper Pizazz™)
6 Christmas lights cards, 6 red envelopes (Cards with Pizazz)
two ⅞" wide wood stars
acrylic paints: golden yellow, white
#2 flat paintbrush, black fine-tip permanent pen
clear Dimensional Magic™ sealer (Plaid Enterprises, Inc.)
five 24" long strands of raffia, glue (see page 8)

Bookmarks by Marilyn Gossett

for each strip bookmark:
glue (see page 8), 1/4" hole punch
pink rose bookmark: 1 1/2"x6 1/4" strip of rose cardstock
(Cards with Pizazz), 1 1/2" square of tan handmade-look
paper (Paper Pizazz™ Handmade Papers)
two 12" lengths of 1/8" wide ivory satin ribbon
black fine-tip pen, 1/2" heart punch (Family Treasures)
decorative scissors (wave by Family Treasures)
snowman bookmark: 1 1/2"x6 1/4" strip of blue cardstock
with snowmen (Cards with Pizazz)
1 1/2" round paper doily
metallic confetti: one 7/8" tall green tree, one 1/4" wide silver star
12" of 1/8" wide ivory satin ribbon
birthday bookmark: 1 1/2"x6 1/4" strip of Happy Birthday
cardstock (Cards with Pizazz)
four 3/8" tall metallic confetti balloons, assorted colors
5/8"x7/8" Happy Birthday! sticker
six 12" long strands of raffia, black fine-tip pen
for each magnetic bookmark:
two 1/2" squares of self-adhesive magnet
rosebud bookmark: 1 3/4"x9" strip of rose-patterned cardstock (Cards with Pizazz)
1/2" heart punch (Family Treasures)
decorative scissors (wave by Family Treasures)
hydrangeas bookmark: 2 1/2"x9" strip of hydrangea cardstock (Cards with Pizazz)
18" of 3/8" wide pink satin picot ribbon

Strip bookmark: Embellish as shown in the photo. Punch
a hole in the center top, 1/2" below the edge. Tie the ribbon
or raffia through the hole.
Magnetic bookmark: Fold the cardstock in half crosswise.
Adhere one magnetic piece to the inside back, 1/2" above the
lower edge, and the other to the matching point on the
inside front. Decorate the front as shown.

Photo Pin & Card

by Anne-Marie Spencer

one 4 1/2"x6 1/4" purple swirl card (Cards with Pizazz)
one 4 1/4"x6" piece of purple sponged paper (Paper Pizazz™)
one 4 1/4"x6" piece of metallic gold paper (Paper Pizazz™)
2/3 yard of 7/8" wide purple/lavender wire-edged ribbon
three 1" long gold oval picture frame charms, photos to fit
one 1 1/4" long pin back
1/4" hole punch, decorative scissors (Victorian by Fiskars®)
gold acrylic paint, makeup sponge
6" of 22-gauge wire, wire cutters, glue (see page 8)

1 **Bow:** Wrap the ribbon around your thumb to make the center loop,
then make a 1 1/2" loop on each side of your thumb. Repeat for another
1 1/2" loop on each side. Bring the ribbon tail up and hold the end behind
the bow center. Insert the wire through the center loop and twist it tightly
on the back of the bow—be sure to catch both ends of the ribbon. Trim the
wire close to the twist. Cut one side of the long back loop close to the wire;
cut the other to 4" long, notching the end in an inverted "V." Glue a photo
to the center of each charm, then glue the charms to the bow tail as
shown. Glue the pin to the back of the bow.

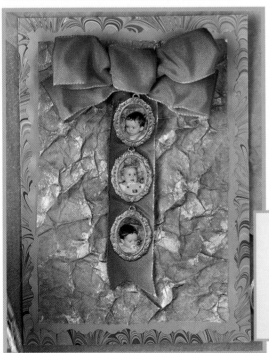

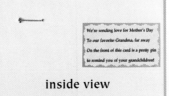

inside view

2 On a flat surface, crinkle the purple
sponged paper tightly. Sponge gold paint
on all the raised surfaces; let dry. Uncrinkle
the paper, then trim to 3 3/4"x5 1/2". Glue to the
gold paper, then use decorative scissors to
trim 1/4" away on all sides. Glue to the card
front. Punch two holes 1 1/4" apart in the center, 1" below the card top. Attach the bow to
the card by pinning it through the holes.

Paper Brooches by Sandy Bunka

basic supplies:
thick tacky craft glue
(optional: also jewelry glue, such as E-6000®,
Goop® or Bond® 527, to glue on the pin back)
1"–1½" long pin back
decorative scissors
metallic gold paint pen
tracing paper, pencil
cardstock or posterboard
specialty papers (see page 7)

1 **Basic instructions:** Glue the specialty paper or papers onto the cardstock. On the back, trace the chosen shape. Use decorative scissors to cut out. If desired, outline the edges with a gold paint pen.

2 Glue down the largest of the decorative elements, then fill in with smaller items such as seed beads. (The glue dries clear, so you don't need to worry about covering it entirely.) Allow to dry overnight, then glue on the pin back.

Heart Brooch

one 1¾" square of cardstock
one 1¾" square of blue giftwrap paper
one ⅞" wide brass basket charm
⅜" wide ribbon roses with ribbon leaves:
 1 dark blue, 1 white
4–6 assorted glass pebble beads, blues and
 purples
20–24 assorted glass seed beads, dark blues
decorative scissors (scallop by Fiskars®)

Seashell Brooch

one 2"x1⅜" piece of cardstock
one 2"x1⅜" piece of ivory parchment paper
one 2"x1⅜" piece of green giftwrap paper
seven ¼"–½" long seashells
1" long sprig of green plastic cedar
eight ¼" long gold glass bugle beads
20–24 glass seed beads, gold and ivory
decorative scissors (Victorian by Fiskars®)

Roughly tear the edges off the green paper and glue it to the center of the trimmed pin, then glue the cedar sprig diagonally over it. Gild the cedar tips with the pen. Follow the basic instructions to attach the shells and beads.

Button Pin

one 2"x1⅜" piece of cardstock
one 2"x1⅜" piece of white watercolor paper
one ½" wide brass open heart charm
4" of 20-gauge gold wire
4" of ⅛" wide wood dowel
three ½"–⅝" wide assorted buttons, browns and golds
three ¼" long seashells
4 burgundy glass pebble beads
20–24 burgundy glass seed beads
decorative scissors (heartbeat by Fiskars®)

Instead of edging the trimmed pin with the gold pen, make random dots and squiggles over the surface. Glue a button and the charm diagonally to the center. Coil the wire around the dowel, bend it slightly and glue it from the upper left to the lower right corner. Glue the remaining buttons into the empty corners, then add the shells and beads.

Corrugated Oval

one 2"x1½" piece of cardstock
one 2"x1½" piece of tan corrugated paper
one ½" long burgundy ribbon rosebud with green ribbon
 leaves
3" of gold curb chain
five ¼"–½" long seashells
four ¼" wide gold squash blossom beads
15–20 gold glass seed beads
decorative scissors (pinking by Fiskars®)

Glue the rosebud and shells in place, then loop and glue the chain among them before adding the remaining beads.

Pin Gift Folders

by Sandy Bunka

Love Folder with Heart Pin

basic supplies (see page 120), metallic gold paint pen
hole punches: 1/8", 1/4"

folder:
pale pink cardstock: one 3"x8 1/2" piece, one 1 5/8"x1" piece
blue cardstock: one 2 1/4" square, one 2"x1 3/8" piece
one 1 7/8"x1 1/4" piece of burgundy handmade paper
one 1/4" wide gold confetti heart
9" of 1/8" wide pink satin ribbon
decorative scissors (ripple by Fiskars®)

pin:
one 1 3/4" square of cardstock
one 1 7/8" square of burgundy handmade paper
20-24 assorted glass seed beads, pink and burgundy
decorative scissors (Victorian by Fiskars®)
brass charms: one 3/4" wide heart, one 3/4" long key
9" of 1/8" wide dark pink satin ribbon

1 **Basic folder:** Fold the large piece of pink cardstock 3 3/4" from each short edge. Bring the short edges together and punch two 1/8" holes 1/2" apart through both layers. After attaching the pin, thread the ribbon ends through the holes, back to front, and tie in a shoestring bow.

2 **Folder front:** Trim the blue, burgundy and pink rectangles with the decorative scissors. Use the pen to edge the cardstock pieces and to write "Love" on the pink piece. Glue the cardstock pieces and confetti heart to the folder front as shown. **Inside plaque:** Edge the blue square with the scissors and pen. Hold in place on the inside back of the folder, 1" below the top edge, and punch two 1/4" holes 1" apart through both layers. Follow step 3 to make the pin, then pin in place through both layers, securing the blue square.

3 **Pin:** Use the heart pattern on page 120 and follow the basic instructions. Tear the burgundy paper into a heart and glue to the cardstock; edge with the gold pen and let dry. After attaching the charms and beads, tie the ribbon into a shoestring bow with 1/2" loops and 1" tails; glue to the center top.

Blue Folder with Rose Pin

basic supplies (see page 120)
decorative scissors (heartbeat by Fiskars®)
folder: one 3"x8 1/2" piece of blue cardstock
one 2"x2 1/4" piece of tan parchment cardstock
light blue cardstock: one 2"x2 1/2" piece, one 1 1/2"x1" piece
9" of 1/8" wide dark blue satin ribbon
black fine-tip pen
pin: one 1 3/4"x1 1/8" piece of white cardstock
one 2 1/4"x1 1/8" piece of white handmade paper
one 1 1/2" long blue paper rose
four 1/4" wide shell or stone chips

Use the blue cardstock to make a folder (step 1 above). Edge the remaining pieces with scissors and gold ink. Use the large light blue piece for the inside plaque (step 2 above), placing the holes vertically in the center. Glue the others to the front as shown; write "For You" in black. **Pin:** Crinkle the handmade paper as you glue it to the cardstock; edge with decorative scissors. Glue the rose and pin back vertically; glue the chips along the bottom.

Black Folder with Beehive Pin

basic supplies (see page 120), eight 9" long strands of raffia
folder: one 3"x8 1/2" piece of black cardstock
tan parchment cardstock: one 2"x2 1/4" piece, one 2 1/4"x1 3/8" piece, one 2 1/4"x1/2" strip
one 1/4" wide gold confetti heart
pin: one 1 1/2"x1 5/8" piece of white cardstock
one 1 1/2"x4" piece of tan corrugated paper
one 1/2" square of black cardstock
one 5/8" long resin bee
decorative scissors (Victorian by Fiskars®)

Use the black cardstock to make a folder (step 1 above). Use three raffia lengths instead of ribbon for the tie. Edge the top edge of the parchment strip and both parchment rectangles with scissors and gold ink. Use the large rectangle for the inside plaque (step 2 above). Glue the others to the front as shown. **Pin:** Cut a large hive from white cardstock and corrugated, a medium and a small hive from corrugated, and a door from black cardstock. Glue as shown. Tie the remaining raffia into a shoestring bow with 1" loops and 1 1/2" tails; glue the bee and bow to the hive top

Gifts, Presents & Splendid Surprises - 121

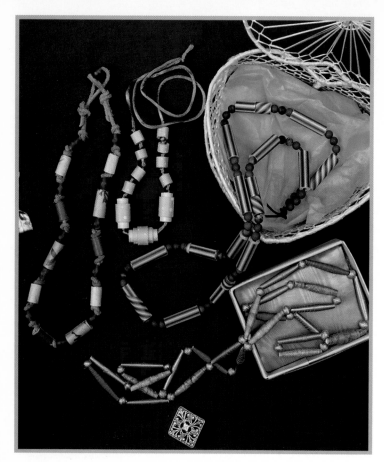

Paper Bead Necklaces
by LeNae Gerig

for each bead:
3" of ⅛" wide wood dowel
glue (see page 8)
clear nail polish

1 Cut paper strips as instructed in the project directions.

2 Roll each strip around the dowel; glue the end and let dry. Carefully slide off the dowel. Brush a thin coat of clear nail polish over the bead and let dry. The polish will protect the bead from moisture and the oils from your skin.

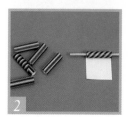

Suede Choker

papers: one 8½"x11" sheet of tan handmade-look, one 8½"x11" sheet of brown handmade-look, one 8½"x11" sheet of tan handmade-look with cedar (Paper Pizazz™ Handmade Papers)
twelve 10mm transparent brown plastic beads
1 yard of 2mm (⅛") brown suede leather cord

Cut three ¾"x11" strips of pine needle paper. Cut four ½"x11" tan and three ½"x11" brown paper strips. Follow the directions above to make the strips into beads. String the paper and plastic beads as shown, knotting between beads. **Clasp:** Thread a bead onto one end and make a 1" loop; knot to secure. On the opposite end make a loop just big enough to go over the bead; knot to secure.

Blue and Brown Necklace

papers: one 8½"x11" sheet of blue corrugated-look, one 8½"x11" sheet of brown corrugated-look (Paper Pizazz™ Country)
forty-eight 6mm brown matte glass beads
⅔ yard of 1.5mm (1/16") black leather cord

Cut eight 1"x11" strips of brown paper and seven of blue. Follow the directions above to roll a bead from each strip. String the beads on the cord, alternating colors with groups of 2–3 glass beads as shown until all are used. Knot the cord ends together.

Green & Peach Necklace

papers: one 8½"x11" sheet of mint with white dots, one 8½"x11" sheet of peach with white dots, one 8½"x11" sheet of peach/mint plaid, one 8½"x11" sheet of peach with pastel dots (Paper Pizazz™ Light Great Backgrounds)
⅔ yard of ⅛" wide mint satin cord

Cut five ¼"x11" mint dotted strips and three ¾"x11" plaid strips. Cut four ¼"x11" strips of peach with white dots and three ½"x11" strips of peach with pastel dots. Follow the directions above to make the plaid strips into beads. Roll a ½" strip around each plaid bead. Roll a mint strip around one of the layered beads. Make each remaining strip into a bead. Thread onto the center of the cord as shown, knotting between beads. Knot the necklace ends together.

Purple & Gold Necklace

papers: one 8½"x11" sheet of purple sponged, one 8½"x11" sheet of purple moiré, one 8½"x11" sheet of purple swirl (Paper Pizazz™ Pretty Papers), one 8½"x11" sheet of metallic gold (Paper Pizazz™ Metallic Papers)
⅔ yard of gold beading cord
twenty-four 8mm gold textured beads

Follow the pattern to cut twelve gold triangles and four triangles each of the sponged, moiré and swirl papers. Starting at the base of the triangle, roll each paper around the dowel; glue the triangle point down and let dry. Seal with polish and let dry. String as shown, alternating with the gold beads. Knot the thread ends together, pulling them tight so the beads form a continuous loop.

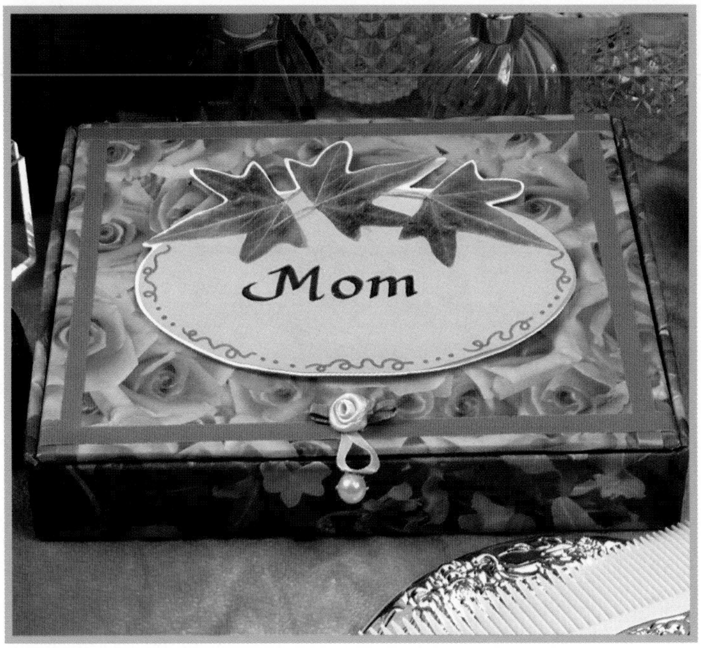

Fern Box & Cards

by Katie Hacker

one 7"x2"x5" papier-mâché book box
papers: three 8½"x11" sheets of fern handmade-look, one 8½"x11" sheet of ivory handmade-look, one 8½"x11" sheet of green handmade-look paper (Paper Pizazz™ Handmade Papers), four 8½"x11" sheets of green, one 8"x1½" strip of green
four 6¼"x4½" fern handmade-look cards (Cards with Pizazz)
8" of 2" wide green/blue paper ribbon
1¼ yards of green twine, one 8½" long twig
six ¼"-½" assorted wood or wood-look beads
spray adhesive, tacky craft glue

1 **Box:** Spray the back of a fern sheet with adhesive. Smooth onto the box top. Fold the edges under, folding out the excess at the corners. Cut an 8½"x4" piece of fern paper and spray it. Set the box bottom on it 1" from the front edge. Fold the edges up onto the box, folding out the excess at the corners. Cut an 8"x4½" piece and glue over the front edge, folding it to the inside. Cut two 5"x4½" pieces and glue one onto each side. Cut a 6"x11" piece; glue to the inside lid and box bottom.

2 Glue the paper ribbon across the box top, wrapping the ends under. Crinkle the green paper strip into a ball, unfold and glue over the ribbon. Tear an 8"x¾" ivory strip, crinkle, unfold and glue over the green strip. Cut an 8" twine length and a 2¾" twig length. Knot the twig in the twine center, then add two beads on each side. Glue over the ivory strip. Glue a ½" bead to the box lid front, turning the hole horizontal. Glue another bead to the box front just below the one on the lid. Tie a 5" twine length through the top bead and slip it over the bottom bead to close the box.

Mom's Box

by Katie Hacker

one 7"x6"x1" papier-mâché box
papers: two 8½"x11" sheets of pink rosebuds, two 8½"x11" sheets of ivy (Paper Pizazz™ Floral Papers), one 2"x8" strip of metallic gold paper (Paper Pizazz™ Metallic Papers), one 3½"x5½" piece of pink, one 3½"x5½" piece of white
3 ivy leaf cutouts (Paper Pizazz™ Embellishments)
2" of ⅛" wide pink satin ribbon
one ½" wide pink ribbon rose with ribbon leaves
one ¼" white pearl bead
5¼" long oval template, pencil
black calligraphy pen, metallic gold pen
foam mounting tape, spray adhesive, tacky craft glue

1 Cut a 9"x7½" piece of rosebuds paper. Glue to the box top. Glue the edges under, folding out the excess at the corners. Cut a 6½" square and glue to the inside lid, covering the edges. Spray the back of an ivy sheet and set the box on it. Fold the edges up the sides and into the box. Cut a 8¾"x7½" piece of ivy paper. Fold the edges in 1", then cut out the squares made by the fold lines in each corner. Glue the piece into the box bottom, turning the edges up.

2 Cut two ¼"x6½" and two ¼"x7½" gold paper strips. Glue ⅜" from the box lid edges as shown. Cut a pink oval; glue the ivy leaves to it as shown. Glue to a piece of white paper and trim 1/16" away. Use the black pen to write "Mom" in the center of the oval. Use the gold pen to draw a border of dots and squiggles. Use foam tape to attach to the box lid. Glue the pearl to the box side. Form the ribbon into a loop to fit over the pearl; glue the ends to the box top and the rose over them.

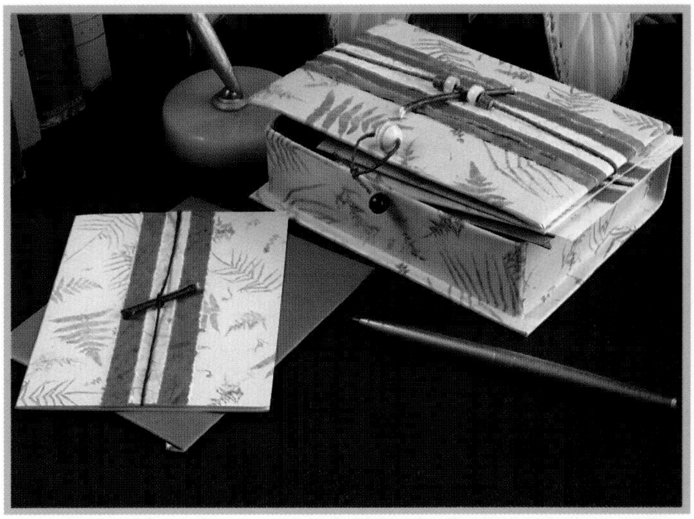

3 **For each card:** Tear a 1½"x5⅝" handmade-look green strip; glue to the center front. Tear a ½"x5⅝" ivory strip and glue it over the green. Cut a 6½" twine length, knot a 1½" twig piece in the center and glue over the ivory. Trim the excess. Use green paper to make an envelope (see page 15) for each card.

Pretty Paper Party Favors

You're feeling festive! Invitations are being made, cakes are baking in the oven, crêpe paper is streaming from the ceilings and you're looking for that one thing that will make this party as unique as the person being celebrated. This chapter was designed with just those thoughts in mind and boy, do we have some answers for you!

Homemade party favors bring a one-of-a-kind aspect to any party. Make a centerpiece from a bit of tulle, a placemat doily, some potpourri and a gold charm for a wedding reception. The project is inexpensive, keeping this favor economical enough to place on every table in the hall. This chapter also teaches four styles of favor boxes (pages 126–128). You can tailor each style to the specific occasion by simply substituting appropriate cardstock patterns. What is put inside will add to the fun as each guest has the excitement of opening his or her own little present.

Lengths of paper ribbon and tulle are crafted into wrap-up party favors. You choose what's to be inside, from potpourri to candy to colored rice. How about filling them with painted macaroni for a child's party, then using the noodles for a party craft activity? Each pouch can be embellished with just the right accents for your occasion.

These designs are simple, and very cost-effective, yet fresh enough to bring that sense of uniqueness to any shindig you throw!

Triangle Boxes
by Caryl McHarney

Cute little boxes, just the right size for trinkets or candy, can sit at a place setting, hang on a tree or top a package.

for each box:
one 4½"x6¼" piece of cardstock
tracing paper, pencil, stylus, ruler
needle with a large eye (like a tapestry needle)
⅛" hole punch, glue (see page 8)

Trace the pattern, place it on the back side of the cardstock and trace around it. Cut out. Use the ruler and stylus to score along the fold lines. Punch holes in two corners as shown on the pattern. Fold into a pyramid, with the flaps inside. Fill with treats or a small gift, then glue the flaps in place. (*Tip:* If you use repositionable glue, the box can be opened without destroying it and easily reclosed.) Use the needle to thread decorative ribbon or raffia through the holes.

happy birthday box:
½ of a happy birthday card (Cards with Pizazz)
9" of ⅛" wide green satin ribbon

Tie the ribbon in a shoestring bow with ¾" loops and 2" tails. Knot the end of each tail.

wedding box:
½ of a diagonal ribbons card (Cards with Pizazz)
16" of ⅟₁₆" wide cream satin ribbon
⅝" wide gold heart charm

Cut the ribbon in half and hold the lengths together to thread them through the holes, catching the loop of the charm. Tie a shoestring bow with ¾" loops and 1½" tails. Knot the end of each tail.

Christmas box:
½ of a Christmas candy card (Cards with Pizazz)
9" of ¼" wide white satin ribbon

Tie the ribbon in a shoestring bow with 1" loops and 1" tails.

baby box:
½ of a pastel quilt card (Cards with Pizazz)
9" of ¼" wide light blue satin ribbon

Follow the directions above to make the box. Thread the ribbon through the box holes and tie a shoestring bow with 1" loops and tails.

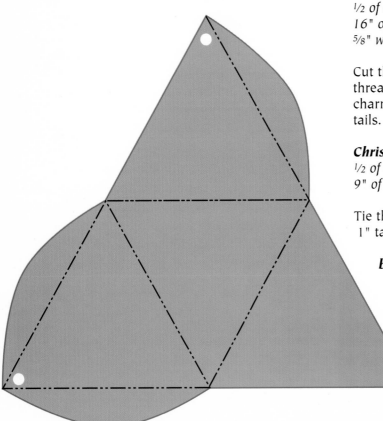

Birdhouse Box

by Caryl McHarney

4¹⁄₂"x6¹⁄₄" barnwood card (Cards with Pizazz)
12" of ⁵⁄₈" wide peach wire-edged ribbon
round wood toothpick, wire cutters
tracing paper, pencil, craft knife, stylus, ruler, glue (see page 8)

1 Trace the tan roof and house patterns (ignore the green lines). Place the house pattern on the inside front of the card, positioning the knothole on the center bottom front behind the gray circle. Trace around it. Trace the roof on the inside card back. Cut out. Use the ruler and stylus to score along all fold lines.

2 Fold the walls and glue the flaps inside the house. Use the knife to cut two slits in the roof as shown by the heavy lines; make a small hole in the center front of the house below the knothole. Cut a ¹⁄₂" length of toothpick and glue into the hole for a perch.

3 Place the roof on the house and run ribbon down through one slit, around the bottom of the house and up through the slit on the opposite side. Tie the ribbon in a shoestring bow with 1¹⁄₄" loops and 1¹⁄₂" tails.

Use the tan and gray lines for the Birdhouse Box.

Use the green lines for the Christmas House Box.

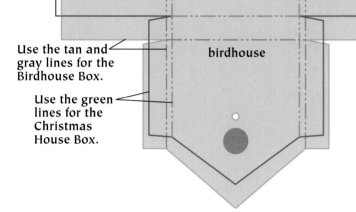

birdhouse

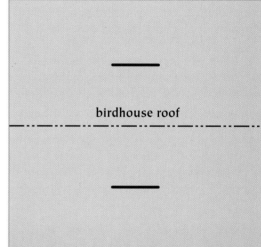

birdhouse roof

Christmas House Box

by Caryl McHarney

Christmas house roof

¹⁄₂ of a red/green striped card, ¹⁄₂ of a Christmas candy card (Cards with Pizazz)
12" of ¹⁄₈" wide red satin ribbon
Christmas toys stickers (©Mrs. Grossman's Paper Co.)

Follow the directions above, using the green lines on the house pattern and the green roof pattern; omit the perch. Place the stickers on the front of the house and tie the ribbon into a shoestring bow with 1" loops and tails.

Heart Basket & Box

by Marilyn Gossett

for each favor:
decorative scissors (wave by Family Treasures)
low temperature glue gun and sticks or thick tacky craft glue
floral basket:
1 pink roses card (Cards with Pizazz)
24" of ³⁄₈" wide metallic gold grosgrain ribbon
10" of 6" wide white tulle
2 Tbsp. of potpourri
purple box:
2 purple hydrangeas cards (Cards with Pizazz)
one 1¹⁄₂" wide paper doily
one 1¹⁄₂" wide brass angel charm
9" of ³⁄₈" wide pink satin picot ribbon

1 **Basket:** Open the card flat and use the decorative scissors to cut a 2¹⁄₂"x9" strip. Using the scored fold for the bottom point, shape the strip into a heart and glue to secure. Handle: Use the patterned scissors to cut a ³⁄₄"x6" strip from the remaining card. Glue a 6" ribbon length to the center. Glue the ends inside the basket as shown.

2 Base: Set the heart on the blank side of the remaining card piece, ¹⁄₂" from the edges, and trace around it. Cut away with the decorative scissors. Turn right side up. Apply a bead of glue to the bottom edges of the basket and press onto the base.

3 Glue a 9" length of ribbon ³⁄₈" below the basket top, beginning between the heart shoulders. Use the remaining ribbon to make a shoestring bow with 1" loops and 1¹⁄₂" tails. Glue to the top of the handle. Line the basket with tulle and fill with potpourri.

4 **Purple box:** Follow steps 1–2 to make the box, but trim ¹⁄₄" off each end of the card strip before shaping into a heart, to ensure that the box will be smaller than the lid. Omit the handle. Follow steps 1–2 to make the lid, but cut the strip only 1" wide. Glue the ribbon around the lid sides just below the top. Glue the doily and charm to the lid top.

Pink Round Box

by Marilyn Gossett

one 2³⁄₄"x1³⁄₄" round papier-mâché box
papers: one 8¹⁄₂"x11" piece of pink moiré (Paper Pizazz™ Wedding), one
   8¹⁄₂"x11" piece of pink roses (Paper Pizazz™ Holidays & Seasons)
decorative scissors (deckle by Fiskars®)
two 6" lengths of ¹⁄₈" wide pink satin ribbon
ribbon roses: one ¹⁄₂" wide pink, one 1" wide dark pink ruffled
pencil, glue (see page 8)

1 Lay the moiré paper right side up; trace around the box top and bottom. Cut out the circles and glue in place. Cut 1¹⁄₂"x10" strip of pink moiré and glue around the box; glue a ¹⁄₂"x9" strip around the lid. Cut a ¹⁄₄"x10" strip of roses paper, trim one edge with the decorative scissors and glue around the top of the lid sides. Repeat with a ³⁄₈" wide strip around the box bottom.

2 Use decorative scissors to cut two 11"x1¹⁄₂" pieces of rose paper; fold each widthwise into ¹⁄₂" pleats and pinch one side to make a paper fan. Fold under the pinched ends and glue to the box lid, back sides together. Cross the ribbon lengths and glue in front of the fans. Glue the roses to the crossed ribbons.

Pink Lace Purse

by Marilyn Gossett

one 5½"x9" piece of pink lace paper (Paper Pizazz™ Pretty Papers)
white paper doilies: one 6" square, one 3" round
one 1" long pink paper rose
three ⅛" wide clear acrylic rhinestones
8" of ⅜" wide mauve satin picot ribbon
12" of gold shredded metallic ribbon
double-stick tape, glue (see page 8)

1 Fold each long edge of the paper under ¼". Fold in half, right sides together, then fold each half down, measuring ¼" away on each side from the first fold, making a pleat. Glue the edges together above the pleat. Cut the square doily in two, then fold under 1" along each cut edge. Slip the fold of one over the top edge of the purse and glue the cut edge to the inside; repeat on the opposite side.

2 Glue the ribbon ends inside the purse for a handle. Cut the round doily in half and fold into ¼" pleats. Pinch into a fan and glue to the purse front. Glue the rose to the center of the fan, then glue the rhinestones to the petals and leaves. Use the shredded ribbon to make a shoestring bow with 1" loops and 4" tails; glue above the rose.

Bridal Lace Sachet

by Marilyn Gossett

one 12" square white paper doily
1 yard of 6" wide white tulle
six ¾" round metallic gold paper doilies
one 1¼" wide white plastic dove
one 1" wide white organdy rose
¼ cup of potpourri
glue (see page 8)

1 Fold the edges of the doily under ½", then fold the points in to the center. Fill with potpourri and glue the edges together as shown. Glue a gold doily at the top of each point.

2 Wrap tulle around the sachet. Gather at the top; tie in a shoestring bow with 2" loops and 2" tails. Glue the last two doilies back to back behind the bow, the rose in front and the dove in the center.

Paper Ribbon Angel

by Marilyn Gossett

4" wide blue/white checked twisted paper ribbon: 12" length,
  6" length
3" of 4" wide pink/white checked twisted paper ribbon
12" of 6" wide white tulle
20" of 1" wide green organza ribbon with gold edges
one 1 1/2" long sprig of three 3/4" wide violet paper flowers
three 1" long sprigs of three 1/2" wide purple silk flowers
two 1" long sprigs of blue/white silk marshberries
one 1" wide covered button doll face
1/4 cup of potpourri
decorative scissors (mini pinking by Fiskars®)
pink powdered blush, cotton swab
glue (see page 8)

1 Untwist all the paper ribbon except the 6" length. Lay the tulle on the inside of the 12" paper ribbon length. Place the potpourri in the center of the tulle. Wrap the sides of the tulle over the potpourri, then gather the tulle and paper ribbon together above the potpourri. **Apron:** Use the decorative scissors to trim the top and bottom edges of the pink/white paper ribbon. Hold it in the center front of the sachet and wrap the green ribbon tightly twice around the sachet, 1" below the apron top. Tie in back in a shoestring bow with 2" loops and 2" tails.

2 **Arms:** Knot the center of the 6" twisted ribbon length for hands. Tuck and glue the ends under the apron just below the tie. Fold down the top edge of the pink ribbon for a collar. Glue the button face above the fold; blush the cheeks. Cut 1/4" wide fringe in the blue ribbon around the face. Glue the flowers into her arms as shown.

Paper Ribbon Bath Sachet

by Marilyn Gossett

10" of 4" wide blue/white checked twisted paper ribbon,
  untwisted
10" of 6" wide white tulle
20" of 1" wide green organza ribbon with gold edges
one 1 1/2" long sprig of three 3/4" wide violet paper flowers
one 1 1/2" long sprig of three 1/2" wide purple silk flowers
1/4 cup of bath salts, glue (see page 8)

This sachet filled with bath salts is a simpler version of the paper ribbon angel. Gather the tulle around the salts, wrap in the paper ribbon and tie with the organza ribbon. Glue the flowers as shown.

Other ideas: Use Halloween print ribbon and fill with candy for trick-or-treats; use a Santa doll face on red ribbon for a Christmas table favor.

Birthday Bunny
by Marilyn Gossett

one 8" square of ivory cardstock
one 2"x3½" piece of purple plaid paper (Paper Pizazz™)
1 balloon cutout (Paper Pizazz™ Birthday)
wood pieces: one 3" wide heart, one ¾" tall spool
white pom poms: one 1" wide, one ⅜" wide
three 1" long Christmas packages wrapped in foil
ribbon roses: two 1" wide pink, one ½" wide white, one ½" wide blue
1 pink ribbon bow with ½" loops and ¾" tails (or use a 9" length of ¼" wide pink satin ribbon and tie your own)
2" of multi-colored star garland
one 36" long strand of raffia
black fine-tip pen
pink powdered blush, cotton swab
dark green acrylic paint
one ½" wide flat paintbrush
tracing paper, pencil, glue (see page 8)

1 Cut out the balloons, glue to the cardstock and trim ⅛" away. Trace the bunny pattern and cut from cardstock; trace the hat and cut from plaid paper. Paint the heart and spool green; let dry.

2 Use the pen to draw the bunny's face; blush the cheeks, inner ears, arms and tummy. Glue the bow under the chin. Glue the hat to the bunny's head. Glue the ⅜" pom pom to the top of the hat. Glue one package to her hand.

hat

3 Wrap the garland around the paintbrush handle to coil it. Wrap one end around the bunny's right hand, then glue the other end to the back of the balloons. Reinforce by gluing a 2" square of plaid paper over the garland ends. Glue the 1" pom pom for a tail.

4 Glue the bunny to the heart base, then reinforce by gluing the spool behind the bunny. Glue the packages and ribbon roses to the base as shown. Cut the raffia into three 12" lengths, hold together and tie a shoestring bow with 1" loops and 8" tails. Glue to the bottom balloon.

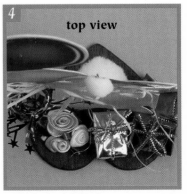

3
back view

4
top view

Rubber Stamping & Fun for Everyone

If you're a fan of rubber stamps, you'll love the projects in this chapter. The crafts offered here give new ideas for incorporating rubber stamps into paper crafts. There are also some great techniques for paint sponging, masking and the three-dimensional effects that can be achieved with stamps. If you're new to rubber stamping, this chapter also provides tried and true tips for basic stamping techniques. There's never been a better time to learn!

Stamped window cards provide an opportunity to stamp the inside of the card as well as the outside. The window lets you see both at a glance! A variation of this could be to mat the window for more detail in the card. Combining stamped images to create a scene is an excellent chance to use all of your favorite stamps in the same project (the masking technique on page 134 shows how). Another great way to incorporate many stamps in one image is shown with the Tree in the Window card on page 136). These are just a few of the ideas you'll find in this chapter.

Rubber stamp images can be used to enhance the ideas you want your project to convey. This chapter shows the specific stamping techniques you'll use to create effects that will be treasured for a lifetime as something made from the goodness of your heart.

Stamping Basics

Be careful to press the stamp **firmly** and **evenly** onto the stamp pad surface, then **firmly** and **evenly** onto the paper. Rocking the stamp will cause the image to blur. Color in your image if you wish, using colored pencils or watercolor pens.

1 To use more than one color on the same stamp, or if the color or you want is not available in an ink pad, use watercolor pens to color directly on the rubber stamp.

2 Just before stamping, exhale gently on the stamp to remoisten the ink.

Sponging

Use a small, fine-textured sponge like a makeup sponge. Press it onto a stamp pad or color with watercolor pens. Press it onto the surface to be sponged; repeat as needed. The harder you press, the sharper the edges of the sponged area will be. For a soft look, keep your touch light.

To sponge along the edge of a card, lay it on a protected surface and hold the sponge at an angle so only a small area extends over the card edge. Another technique is to hold the card up and stroke the sponge along the very edge—this produces a soft, narrow border.

Cleaning Rubber Stamps

Stack 3–5 paper towels on a plate and dampen with a solution of one part window cleaner to four parts water. Stamp on the paper towels until all the ink is removed.

Embossing

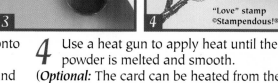

"Love" stamp
©Stampendous!®

1 Stamp the image with embossing ink.

2 Cover the stamped image with embossing powder.

3 Tap off any excess powder onto a sheet of paper. Bend the paper to make a pouring spout and return the powder to the container.

4 Use a heat gun to apply heat until the powder is melted and smooth. (**Optional:** The card can be heated from the underside with an iron on a low setting.)

Masking

- Stamp the image, then stamp it again on scrap paper (or on a sticky note—nice because you won't have to hold it in place). Cut out the image.

- Hold the mask over the first image and stamp again, overlapping the mask. When you remove it, the newly stamped image will appear to be behind the first image.

Cutting Windows

- Lay the card on a cutting mat or protected surface. Hold the craft knife vertically. Use a ruler to cut straight lines. For circles and other shapes, turn the card rather than the knife.
- A circle cutter makes it easy to cut a perfect circle.

- To cut a window with scissors (for example, to cut a patterned edge), first pencil the window shape lightly. Use a knife to cut an X in the window center, then use the scissors to cut around the window.

top view

3-Dimensional Supports

side view

- Cut two cardstock strips 1" wide and ⅛" shorter than the item to be mounted.
- Accordion-fold each in fourths lengthwise. Glue the top folds to the back of the item, one on each side. Glue the bottom folds to the card front or background piece.

Pop-Up Placecard

by Linda Ippel

one 5¹/₂" square of white cardstock
one 5³/₄" square of turquoise plain paper
decorative scissors (zig zag by Family Treasures)
rubber stamps: cupcake, "happy birthday" frame
  (Stampendous!®)
rainbow stamp pad, blue calligraphy pen
watercolor pens: burgundy, red, green
tri-star corner punch (Family Treasures)
craft knife, ruler, pencil, paper towels
glue (see page 8)

1 Use the pencil to lightly mark a horizontal fold line on the center front of the cardstock. Punch each corner. Use the calligraphy pen to write the name above the punched stars on the left card front.

2 Stamp the frame right of the name: Use the rainbow stamp pad and position the frame diagonally so ¹/₃ extends above the fold line. Use the ruler and knife to carefully cut ¹/₈" away from the frame above the fold line. Fold the back of the card down. Use the decorative scissors to trim the cut edge of the pop-up. Line the card with turquoise paper (see page 14).

3 Color the cupcake stamp with the burgundy pen, then stamp in the lower center of the frame. Mask (see page 134) the cupcake. Clean the stamp, color it green and stamp another cupcake to the right, overlapping the mask. Repeat to stamp a red cupcake to the left. Remove the mask.

3-D Birthday Card by Linda Ippel

white cardstock: one 8¹/₂"x5¹/₂" piece, one 4"x8" piece
one 4¹/₄"x5¹/₂" piece of colorful stripes paper (Paper Pizazz™
  Birthday)
rubber stamps: birthday cake, big balloon, mini balloon
  (Stampendous!®)
black stamp pad
watercolor pens: red, orange, yellow, green, blue, purple
colored pencils: light blue, lavender, yellow
self-adhesive foam mounting tape: ¹/₈" thick, ¹/₄" thick
glue (see page 8)

Cover the cardstock with the striped paper (see page 14). Attach the cake and balloons with squares of mounting tape, allowing them to "float" above the card surface.

Postcard Invitation by Linda Ippel

one 5¹/₂"x4¹/₄" piece of white cardstock
one 5¹/₂"x4¹/₄" piece of colorful stripes paper (Paper Pizazz™
  Birthday)
one 5¹/₄"x4" piece of white paper
decorative scissors (zig zag by Family Treasures)
rubber stamps: shadow star, "You are Invited"
  (Stampendous!®)
rainbow stamp pad, glue (see page 8)

Cover the cardstock with the striped paper (see page 14). Stamp the invitation on the white paper, then glue to the card front. Use a different band of the stamp pad to stamp each small star.

Christmas Cheer

by Linda Ippel

one 11"x5½" piece of tan cardstock
rubber stamps: wispy holly, snowflake circle, "Christmas Cheer" (Stampendous!®)
circle cutter or circle template, craft knife, cutting mat
fine iridescent clear glitter
fine-tip pens: red, green, blue, dark blue
stamp pads: green, blue, dark blue
pencil, eraser, glue (see page 8)

Fold the cardstock in half so the opening is on the right; unfold. Cut a 3" circle in the center front, 1" below the top edge. Re-fold the card, then use green ink to stamp a holly border around the outer front. Use red and green pens to color the holly. Use dark blue ink to stamp the snowflakes, then color with both shades of blue pens. Draw dark blue dots of varying sizes among the flakes. Lightly pencil the window onto the inside of the card. Open the card and use green ink to stamp the message inside the circle. Erase the circle and color the holly. Apply glue to the snowflakes and sprinkle on glitter. Let dry, then brush off the excess.

A Tree in the Window

by Linda Ippel

tan cardstock: one 11"x5½" piece, one 5½" square, two 4"x1" strips
rubber stamps: tree stand, gift packages, snowflake, stocking, star, teddy bear, holly button, bells, angel (Stampendous!®)
fine-tip pens: black, blue, red, yellow, green, light blue, brown, magenta, dark yellow
black stamp pad, makeup sponge
corner scissors (nostalgia Corner Edgers by Fiskars®)
six ¼" gold jump rings, six 2" lengths of gold thread
⅛" hole punch (McGill, Inc.), craft knife, cutting mat
pencil, ruler, glue (see page 8)

1 Edge each corner of the cardstock square. Lightly sponge (see page 134) green ink around the outside. Lightly pencil a 3½" square in the center. Stamp the tree stand in the center, overlapping the frame. Use the knife to cut around the tree stand and inside the frame. Stamp a stocking, star, teddy bear, holly button, bell and angel on the cut-out scraps of cardstock. Use the black pen to draw a small bow in each corner, then draw a - - - border ¼" away from the outside of the frame between the bows.

2 Fold the large piece of cardstock in half. Lay the window on the card front and lightly mark the frame with pencil; remove. Stamp packages in the lower ⅓ of the card front, extending above the frame line. Erase any visible pencil lines. Use green ink to stamp snowflakes around the upper window, also extending slightly beyond the marks. Attach the window to

the card front with 3-dimensional supports made from the 4"x1" strips (see page 134).

3 Use the pens to color the stamped ornaments and packages. Cut out the ornaments. Punch holes in the tops and insert a jump ring through each hole. Use thread to tie each ring to a branch of the tree stand; secure with glue.

Garden Angel

by Linda Ippel

tan cardstock: one 8½"x5½" piece, two 4¼"x2¼" pieces
rubber stamps: garden angel, columbine, foxglove, phlox, Queen Anne's lace, Jacob's ladder (Stampendous!®)
fine-tip pens: black, purple, lavender, magenta, violet, blue, green
colored pencils: peach, dark blue, light blue, tan, brown, green, pink, gray, rust, dark yellow
black stamp pad, white paint pen, makeup sponge
3½" oval template, pencil, craft knife, cutting mat
⅛" thick mounting tape

1 Fold the large piece of cardstock in half so the opening is on the right; unfold. Use the pencil to lightly trace the template onto the center front. Use the stamp pad to stamp flowers on both sides of the oval, slightly overlapping it. Mask (see page 134) the first images and stamp other flowers over them. Stamp additional flowers on the remaining cardstock pieces, masking as needed. Use the pens and colored pencils to color the flowers. Cut out the oval window, cutting around the flowers which extend into it. Cut out the other stamped flowers. Use mounting tape to layer the extra flowers on the bottom front of the card.

2 Lightly mark the window outline on the inside of the card. Stamp the angel in the window; color her with pencils for a soft look. Sponge (see page 134) green ink around the card edges. Use the black pen to draw a ——•• —— border around the window. Draw random squiggly lines and dots around the outer top of the card.

I Love You! by Linda Ippel

cardstock: one 8½"x5½" piece of tan, one 4¼"x5½" piece of pale green
"I Love You!," sword fern, lavender, cyclamen rubber stamps (Stampendous!®)
stamp pads: green, red, black
decorative scissors (deckle by Family Treasures)
corner punch (Family Treasures)
fine-tip pens: black, green, blue, pink, red
2¾" and 2½" circle templates, craft knife, cutting mat, pencil, ruler
makeup sponge, glue (see page 8)

Like the Garden Angel above, this card has stamped images overlapping the window. A matted effect was created by lining the card front with slightly darker cardstock and cutting a smaller window in it. The corner punches and deckle trim on the lower edge let the lining show.

Thank You

by Linda Ippel

cardstock: one 8½"x5½" piece of pink, one 4¼"x5½" piece of light green, one 4½"x5½" piece of tan
rubber stamps: "Thank You," country chair, aster (Stampendous!®)
corner punch (fleur de lis by Family Treasures)
fine-tip pens: black, green, purple, gold, pink, brown
stamp pads: green, black ; colored pencils: brown, yellow, blue
makeup sponge, craft knife, cutting mat, pencil, ruler, glue (see page 8)

The same matting technique used for the "I Love You!" card at left makes this card with a square window. Tan and green layers glued to the pink card front create a subtle color transition.

Vellum-Lined Windows

by Linda Ippel

for each card:
pencil
glue (see page 8)

Poppy Card:

one 8"x5½"" piece of orange cardstock
one 4"x5½" piece of peach paper
one 4"x5½" piece of vellum
black fine-tip pen, black stamp pad
watercolor pens: orange, red, green
poppy rubber stamp (RubberStampede®)
oval template, craft knife, cutting mat

Fold the orange cardstock in half. Trace the oval onto the front, then open the card and cut out the window. Stamp the poppies onto the center of the vellum; let dry. Use watercolor pens to color the image. Glue the vellum to the inside card front, then glue the peach paper behind the vellum. Use the black pen to draw a —— •• —— border around the window, then draw a wavy line over each ——.

Nasturtium Card:

one 5½"x8" piece of blue cardstock
one 5½"x4" piece of peach paper
one 5½"x3" piece of vellum
ruler, red fine-tip pen, colored pencils: peach, red, green
nasturtium rubber stamp (RubberStampede®)
embossing ink pad
white embossing powder
heat gun
¼" and ½" heart punches (Family Treasures)

Fold the blue cardstock in half to open at the bottom. Open the card and cut a 4⅝"x2¼" window in the lower front. Punch a row of hearts above the window as shown. Emboss (see page 134) the nasturtiums onto the center of the vellum. Use pencils to color the image. Glue the vellum to the inside card front, then glue the peach paper behind the vellum. Use the red pen to draw a —— // —— border around the window. Draw squiggly lines and dots between the hearts as shown.

Apple Harvest

by Linda Ippel

apple farm rubber stamp (Stampendous!®)
cardstock: one 5¹/₂"x4" piece of tan corrugated
(MPR Paperbilities™), one 5¹/₂"x4" piece of
red, one 5¹/₂"x8" piece of dark blue, two 4"x1"
pieces of tan
fine-tip pens: red, green
colored pencils: tan, white, green
black stamp pad, pencil, ruler, craft knife
decorative scissors (deckle by Family Treasures)
glue (see page 8)

1 Measure and lightly mark a ¹/₂" border along the right top, side and bottom of the card. Use the black ink pad to stamp the red card; let dry. Use the pens and colored pencils to color the image. Cut away the card between the stamped image and the marked border as shown. Trim the outer edges with decorative scissors.

2 Use the 4"x1" strips to make support pieces (see page 134) to attach the window to the corrugated piece. Fold the blue cardstock in half to open at the bottom. Glue the corrugated to the front of the blue card.

Wheelbarrow Card by Linda Ippel

old wheelbarrow stamp (Stampendous®)
cardstock: one 5¹/₂"x4" piece of brown, one 5¹/₂"x8" of yellow,
two 4"x1" pieces of yellow
black stamp pad. craft knife, cutting mat, 4¹/₂" oval template, pencil
fine-tip pens: black, blue, brown, green, yellow, purple, violet, lavender, red
decorative scissors (deckle by Family Treasures), glue (see page 8)

This card uses an oval window rather than a rectangle, and the support pieces are glued directly to the card front; the construction is the same as for the card above.

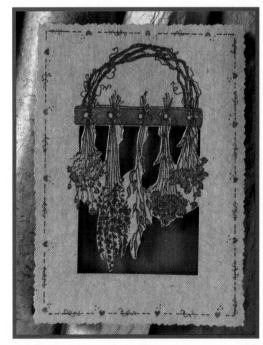

Dried Flowers Card

by Linda Ippel

drying flowers stamp (Stampendous!®)
cardstock: one 5¹/₂"x4" piece of brown, one 5¹/₂"x8" piece of dark green,
two 4"x1" pieces of brown
black stamp pad, craft knife, cutting mat, ruler, pencil
fine-tip pens: black, magenta, green, blue, yellow, orange, brown, purple
decorative scissors (deckle by Family Treasures)
glue (see page 8)

Another card made like the Apple Harvest card has a hand-drawn border of multi-colored hearts, dashes and squiggles which pick up the colors of the hanging flowers to make it especially charming.

Seashore Thanks

by Linda Ippel

tan cardstock: one 12"x7¹⁄₈" piece, two 1³⁄₈"x1⁵⁄₈"
    pieces, two 1¹⁄₂"x1³⁄₄" pieces, one 2⁵⁄₈"x1³⁄₄" piece,
    three 1" squares
one 3"x2" piece of brown corrugated cardboard (MPR
    Paperbilities™)
rubber stamps: "Thanks!!!", anchor, sailboat, wave
    frame, ocean floor, seashore scene (Stampendous!®)
decorative scissors (ripple by Fiskars®)
punches: ¹⁄₂" scallop shell, ¹⁄₄" star, corner rounder
    (Marvy® Uchida), ¹⁄₈" and ¹⁄₄" round (McGill, Inc.)
28" long raffia strands: 1 teal, 3 tan
watercolor pens: green, aqua, teal
fine-tip pens: red, dark blue, brown
colored pencils: tan, brown, pink, light blue
black stamp pad, glue (see page 8)

1 Color the ocean floor stamp with watercolor
pens; stamp into the lowest 1¹⁄₄" of the large
cardstock piece, masking the images as necessary
(see page 134). Color the frame stamp with the
watercolor pens, using green on the left side, aqua in the
center and teal on the right. Stamp in the center of the cardstock, ¹⁄₂" above the ocean floor. Use black to stamp the
seashell scene in the frame center. Color the scene.

2 Trim the top edge of the cardstock with decorative scissors. Fold as shown in the diagram; glue the back seam
and the bottom flaps. Gently pinch the top sides of the bag
to close it. Punch two ¹⁄₄" holes 2" apart ¹⁄₂" below the bag
top. Insert the raffia lengths through the holes and tie in a
shoestring bow in front. Trim the tails to 6"–12".

3 Sponge (see page 134) the 1¹⁄₂"x1³⁄₄" cardstock pieces
randomly with the watercolor pens. Repeat with the 1"
cardstock squares. Punch three seashells from the squares,
then glue to the lower bag front as shown.

4 Round the corners of the 1³⁄₈"x1⁵⁄₈" and 2⁵⁄₈"x1³⁄₄"
cardstock pieces. Punch each corner of the larger piece
with stars. Color the anchor and sailboat stamps with
watercolor pens and stamp one on each 1³⁄₈"x1⁵⁄₈" piece.
Glue one to each 1¹⁄₂"x1³⁄₄" sponged piece. Sponge the
edges of the 2⁵⁄₈"x1³⁄₄" piece with teal, then color the
"Thanks!!!" stamp with the pens and stamp in the center.
Glue to the corrugated cardboard. Punch a ¹⁄₈" hole in each
tag, then tie the tags onto the longest raffia ends.

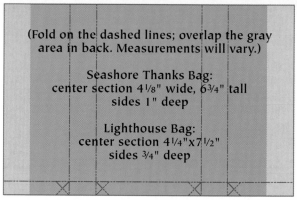

**(Fold on the dashed lines; overlap the gray
area in back. Measurements will vary.)**

Seashore Thanks Bag:
center section 4¹⁄₈" wide, 6³⁄₄" tall
sides 1" deep

Lighthouse Bag:
center section 4¹⁄₄"x7¹⁄₂"
sides ³⁄₄" deep

Lighthouse Bag by Linda Ippel

white cardstock: one 3¹⁄₂"x3³⁄₄" piece, one 4" square,
    five 1" squares
one 12"x8¹⁄₄" piece of dark blue cardstock
decorative scissors (wave by Fiskars®)
angelfish punch (Marvy® Uchida)
watercolor pens: green, aqua, teal
colored pencils: red, light blue, tan, pink, yellow, brown
lighthouse scene rubber stamp (Stampendous!®)
fine iridescent teal glitter, glue (see page 8)

This bag is constructed like the Seashore Thanks bag
above. Sponge (see page 134) multiple "undersea" colors onto the white squares, then punch fish from each
1" square. Turn the 4" square diagonally and glue to the
bag front. Stamp and color the lighthouse scene on the
remaining cardstock piece, trim it with the decorative
scissors and sponge the edges as shown. Glue it over
the sponged paper. Glue the fish as shown, then make
vertical "bubble trails" with glue and iridescent glitter.

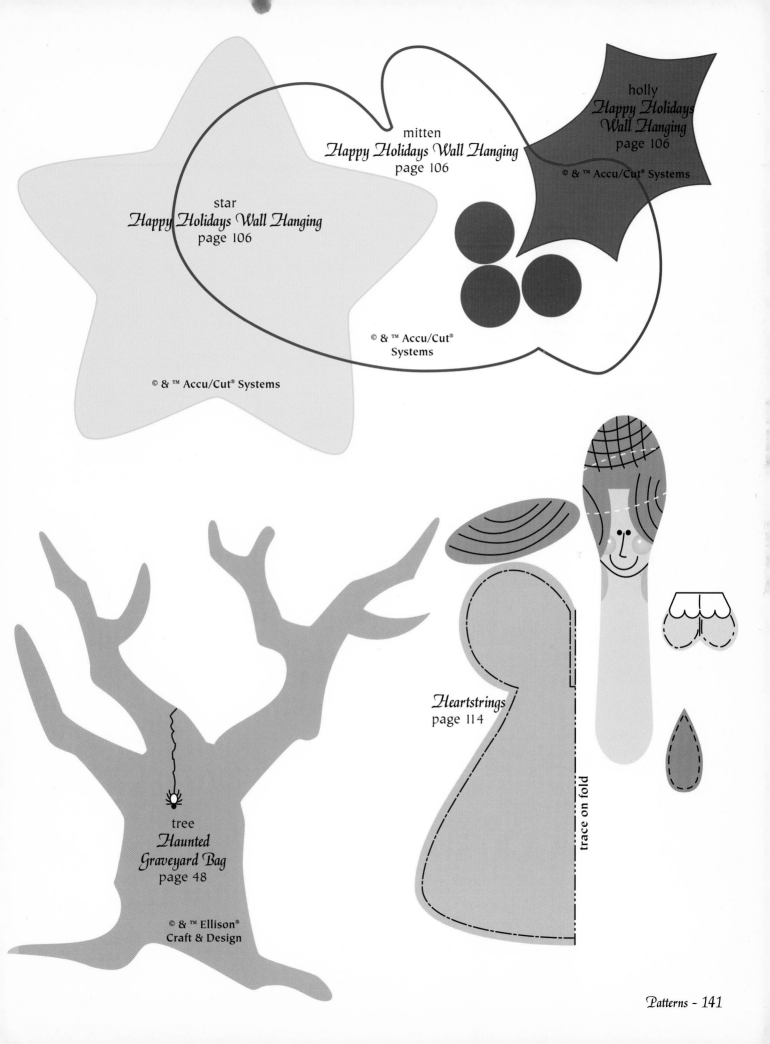

mitten
Happy Holidays Wall Hanging
page 106

holly
*Happy Holidays
Wall Hanging*
page 106

© & ™ Accu/Cut® Systems

star
Happy Holidays Wall Hanging
page 106

© & ™ Accu/Cut®
Systems

© & ™ Accu/Cut® Systems

Heartstrings
page 114

trace on fold

tree
*Haunted
Graveyard Bag*
page 48

© & ™ Ellison®
Craft & Design

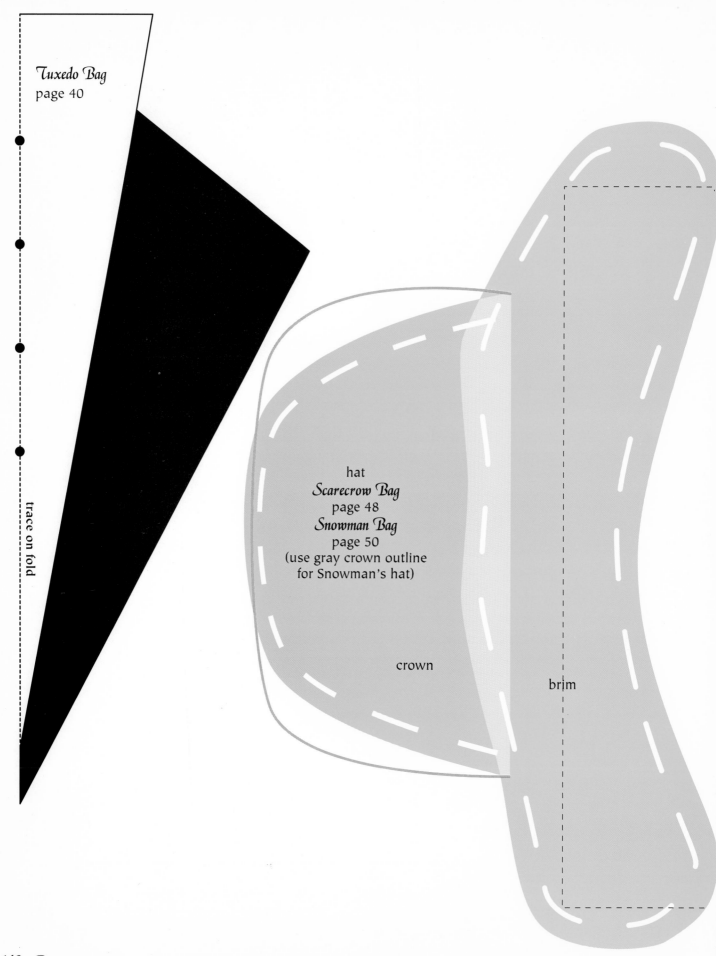

Tuxedo Bag
page 40

trace on fold

hat
Scarecrow Bag
page 48
Snowman Bag
page 50
(use gray crown outline
for Snowman's hat)

crown

brim

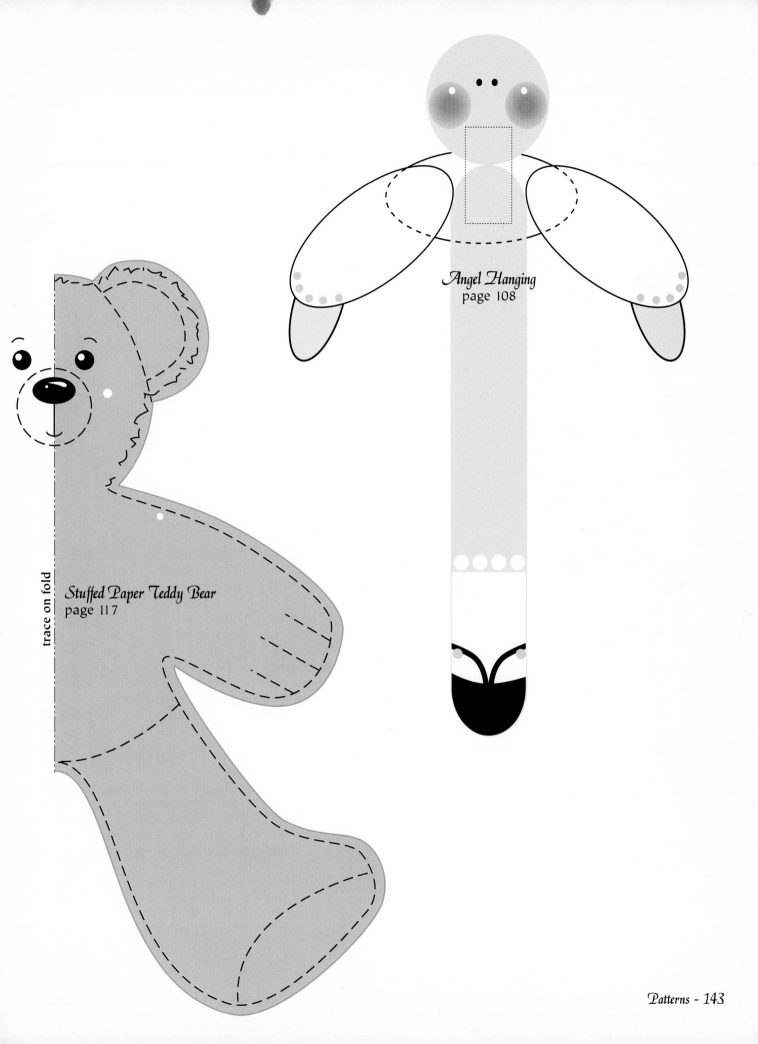

Angel Hanging
page 108

Stuffed Paper Teddy Bear
page 117

trace on fold

Index

• **Chapter Title**　　• Project Title　　• *Technique*

Accordion-Fold Books 90–91
Additionals *10*
Americana Journal. 100
Angel Hanging. 108
Angel Saucer. 69
Angel Topiaries 107
Angel Tree Topper 108
Animal Bags 42–45
Announcement with Lace Envelope . . . 29
Apple Harvest 139
Baby Book. 98
Bi-Fold Ballerina Card 21
Birdhouse Box. 127
Birthday Bunny 131
Books from Cards 92–93
Bookmarks 119
Bow, Shoestring *9*
Boxes from Cards 58–59
Bridal Lace Sachet. 129
Cardstock. *7*
Cards with Die Cuts 24–26
Cheerful, Clever,
　Charming Cards **12–21**
Children's Easy
　Decoupage Dresser Set 70–71
Christmas Bags 49–51
Christmas Cheer 136
Christmas House Box 127
Christmas Wall Cards 106
Cleaning Stamps *134*
Corrugated Box. 73
Corrugated Wall Hanging 73
Corrugator *9*
Covering a Card *14*
Craft Knife *9*
Cream Velvet Box 78
Cutaway Card 21
Cutting Windows *134*
Dainty Doily Pot 68
Decoupage Candle Holder. 67
Decoupage Frames 67
Decoupage Plates 66
Die Cuts *11, 24*
Dresser Set 70–71
Dried Flowers Card 139
Embellished Bags. 40–41
Embellishments *10*
Embossing *134*
Extras *9*
Fall Leaves Hanging 75
Fan Ornaments 109
Fern Box & Cards 123
Fisherman's Brag Book 99
Flat Folders 39
Flower Girl Hangers 113
Garden Angel 137
Gift Folders 62

Gifts, Presents &
　Splendid Surprises **110–123**
Glue *8*
Glue Gun *9*
Gold Crinkle Card 19
Green Wood Frame 82
Halloween Bags. 46–48
Happy Holidays Hanging 106
Haunted Graveyard 48
Haunted House 30
Heart Basket & Box 62
Heart Ornament 105
Holly Leaf Christmas Book 99
Home Decor with
　Style & More **64–83**
Hugs & Kisses 98
Hydrangeas & Cherub 101
I Love You 137
Invitations & Announcements. **22–31**
It's a Boy! 27
It's a Girl! 27
It's in the Bag. **32–53**
Journals & Books **84–101**
Lacy Formals. 28
Lacy Heart Engagement Card 28
Lighthouse Bag 140
Little Fern Book 100
Magnets 83
Making & Covering Cards *14*
Making Envelopes *15*
Masking. *134*
Mini Gift Bags 34–36
Mini Gift Books 86–87
Mini Photo Albums 88–89
Mosiac Fish Tray. 72
Mosiac Terra Cotta Pot 72
Mom's Box 123
Nasturtium Card 138
Nesting Boxes 56–57
Old Letters Scrapbook 96
Paper *6*
Papers, Specialized *7*
Paper Bead Necklaces 122
Paper Brooches 120
Paper Ribbon Angel 130
Paper Ribbon Bath Sachet 130
Paper Rose Projects 80
Paper Treasures &
　Holiday Pleasures **102–109**
Pastel Wall Quilt 75
Patterns **141–143**
Pens *8*
Photo Pin & Card 119
Pin Gift Folders 121
Pink Gingham Frame. 79
Pink Lace Purse 129
Pink Round Box. 128
Pleated Gift Folders 36–39

Pocket Cards 16–17
Pockets Full of Love. 114–115
Poppy Card 138
Pop-Up Party Card 29
Pop-Up Placecard 135
Postcard Invitation 135
Present-Perfect Boxes **54–63**
Pretty Paper Party Favors. . **121–129**
Puffy Ornaments 104
Punches *11*
Punch-Outs™ *11*
Quilted Welcome Wall Hanging. 74
Reverse Decoupage Rose Set 68
Rose Frame 81
Rubber Stamping &
　Fun for Everyone **132–140**
Scissors *8*
Seashore Thanks 140
Seasonal Photo Mats 139
Seed Packet Sachets 112
Shaker Box Cards 18–19
Shaker-Top Boxes 60–61
Shoestring Bow *9*
Snowflake Ornament 109
Specialized Glues *11*
Specialized Papers *7*
Sponging *134*
Square Books 76–77
Square Fold-Ups 63
Stamping *11*
Stamping Basics *134*
Stationery Packets 118
Stickers *11*
Stuffed Paper Ornaments 116–117
Stylus *9*
Sunny Reflections 101
Terrific Tags 52–53
Thank You 137
3-Dimensional Supports. *138*
3-D Cards 20
3-D Birthday Card 135
Tips & Tools **6–11**
Tissue Paper *9*
Tools *8*
To the Sea 96
Tree Box 105
A Tree in the Window 136
Triangle Boxes. 126
Triangle Letter Box 69
Triptych Wall Hanging 82
Vellum-Lined Windows *138*
Velvet Lampshade 79
Victorian Scrapbook 97
Vintage Photo Journal 97
Wheelbarrow Card 139
Windows, Cutting *134*
Wrapping. *10*
X-acto® Knife. *9*